Three Minutes a Day

VOLUME 35

Other Christopher Books in Print

Better to Light One Candle

and other volumes in the

Three Minutes A Day

series

Day by Day with Jesus

God Delights in You

World Religions

THREE MINUTES A DAY
VOLUME 35

The Christophers

Stephanie Raha
Editor-in-Chief

Margaret O'Connell
Senior Research Editor

Joan Bromfield
Jonathan Englert
Monica Yehle-Glick
Robert Michael Morris
Jerry O'Neil
Karen Hazel Radenbough
Anna Marie Tripodi
Ann Marie Welsh
Contributing Editors

The Christophers
12 East 48th Street
New York, NY 10017

Do not be overcome by evil,

but overcome evil with good.

ROMANS 12:21

Introduction

Rev. James Keller, M.M., who started The Christophers in 1945, wrote "that every person without exception has a mission to fulfill. That mission is to bring the light and warmth of God's love to the world."

Father Keller believed that each human being is a potential missionary, wherever he or she may be. He chose the term "Christopher" which comes from the Greek meaning Christ-bearer to describe someone who would bring the principles of the Gospel to the marketplace of everyday life.

The year 2000 is the 100th anniversary of our founder's birth on June 27, 1900.

By the time of Father Keller's death in 1977, The Christophers' message of hope had spread around the world.

Today, we continue to encourage people to believe in–and live by–the ancient Chinese proverb that he chose as our motto: "It's better to light one candle than to curse the darkness."

And we hope that this book will inspire you to light many candles of hope with your life.

The Christophers

Try, Try Again!

There's a certain irony attached to New Year's resolutions. We've all made them, but some of us just cannot manage to accomplish them. Yet, because of their promise of a fresh start, many of us try and try again.

Easy to declare but difficult to carry out, New Year's resolutions are a good way to develop and exercise persistence. In his many books on spirituality, Saint Alphonsus Liguori continually emphasizes the importance of making resolutions. He stresses: even if we forget them or fall short of following through, keep making resolutions.

Here are some tips on keeping your resolutions:

- Make your resolution specific.
- Make your resolution easy, or "do-able."
- Avoid becoming discouraged.
- Tell your resolution to a friend or family member.
- Make your resolution an act of love.

I resolved to live according to Wisdom...and I shall never be disappointed. (Sirach 51:18)

Steer me away from discouraging or disheartening things, Lord, so that I may remain persistent.

Get Moving

How can you be more physically active? Join a gym? With your schedule? Cost is a problem, too.

Bury all remote controls. Eventually you'll learn not to sit for hours.

Move plates and glasses, pot and pans to less accessible shelves unless you have a bad back.

Keep everything needed for exercise in one closet so you'll have no excuse for not wearing, using it.

Leave the treadmill or exercise bike where its presence will haunt you into using it.

Exercise is a life and health enhancing way to care for the gift of your body. Overcome any reluctance to sweat.

Taking good care of yourself means making an effort every day.

God created humankind...in the image of God He created them; male and female He created them. (Genesis 1:27)

Creator, help us to respect ourselves and each other because we have been created in Your likeness.

Murphy's Law—for Beginners

Are you familiar with Murphy's law? If not, here is a list of the simpler things that can and will go wrong.

Leak proof seals—will; self-starters—will not; and interchangeable parts—won't.

Anything you try to fix will take longer and cost more than you thought.

Warranties expire upon payment of the bill.

If it jams—force it; if it breaks, it needed replacement.

The 10¢ fuse will not blow; the $300 picture tube will.

When a broken appliance is demonstrated for the repair person, it will work perfectly. Same goes for crashed or frozen computers. And for absent modem dial tones, scanners that scramble, and fax machines that don't.

There's only one way to survive life's zaniness. Seek the One who gathers each and all of us under His wings.

Cast your burden on the Lord. (Psalm 55:22)

Enable us to seek You, Refuge of the harried and harassed.

Right Time for Decision-making

Life is filled with choices from the mundane to the extraordinary. And timing is big part of any question.

"A decision goes through a life cycle, from infancy to maturity to old age," says Don Paarlberg. "If you make the decision in its infancy, you don't have enough facts. If you wait until it is senile, you have no effect on the outcome. How do you know when a decision is ripe? ...You have to practice decision-making like any other activity."

Kaye Kapsner of Vista, California, says that "making hard decisions was always a struggle for me. Then one day I made a decision, but promised not to act on it until the next day. ...Now I use this approach all the time, and in about ninety percent of cases my day-before decision turns out to be right."

If you are willing to work at decision making like any other skill, you will indeed improve with time and effort.

Before each person are life and death, and whichever one chooses will be given. (Sirach 15:17)

God, show me how to face up to decisions and to know when—and when not to make them.

When You Must Keep Going

Generally, the best thing you can do when you are tired is to rest. Obvious though it may appear, the overworked and frazzled among us sometimes need prodding to get the relaxation and recreation vital to a healthy existence.

There are occasions, however, when what we are doing is so essential that we have to keep going. This does not include the times we stay late at the office finishing a report when we would be better off having dinner with the family.

William James, psychologist and philosopher, observed that, "The fatigue gets worse up to a certain point, then, gradually or suddenly, it passes away and we are fresher than before! We have evidently tapped a new level of energy...We find amounts of ease and power that we never dreamed ourselves to own."

God has entrusted you with great power and potential. Do not be afraid to use it.

How precious is your steadfast love, O God! All people may take refuge in the shadow of Your wings. (Psalm 36:7)

Creator, thank You for giving me so many chances to serve You.

Before You Can Be Great

Marian Anderson's journey to recognition as one of the finest singers of her time was not an easy one.

Born in Philadelphia in 1902, she experienced poverty and racial prejudice. Yet she knew the support of her family and her church in seeking her dream.

One of her earliest appearances, at New York's Town Hall, was a critical disaster. Miss Anderson's depression lasted a year. But her mother never stopped encouraging her. One day she said, "Marian, grace must come before greatness. Why don't you think about this failure a little and pray about it a lot?"

She did. With renewed determination, she got the recognition she deserved both as a celebrated contralto and as a concerned humanitarian.

"Whatever is in my voice," Marian Anderson later said, "faith has put there."

Faith does shape our lives and talents, if we let it.

Whatever you ask for in prayer with faith, you will receive. (Matthew 21:22)

Open my heart to faith, my soul to grace. Never let me shut myself away from You, generous Lord.

Looking to the Future

The beginning of a new year seems like a natural time to make plans and resolutions about where we would like to be in another 365 days. Here are some thoughts on the future that give both encouragement and perspective:

"The future is not the result of choices among alternative paths offered in the present. It is a place...created first in the mind and the will; created next in the activity."–Walt Disney

"Simply to be a human being is to be a futurist of sorts. For human freedom is largely a matter of imagining alternative futures, then choosing among them."–James Ogilvy

"If you won't be better tomorrow than you were today, then what do you need tomorrow for?"–Rabbi Nahman Bratslav

None of us can bend the future to our will. But we can influence it by how we change ourselves, our attitudes, our actions–how we live in the present.

I know the plans I have for you, says the Lord, plans...to give you a future with hope. (Lamentations 29:11)

Help me not to worry about tomorrow, but to live today the way I know is good and right and holy, Spirit of Wisdom.

Selling For His Soul, With His Soul

If there's one thing Owen Bradford Butler could always do, it's sell. His knack for sales propelled him up the corporate ladder at Procter & Gamble to chairman of the board.

Yet, Butler believed he had unfinished business. He put his talent for sales to work to promote and develop what might seem incongruous to a successful, high-profile business executive: early childhood development.

Butler became a passionate advocate for children, speaking out on corporate America's responsibility to support their development. And this truly put his selling skills to the test.

Today, Bright Beginnings, the program he helped create in Colorado, brings more and more newborns and their moms support and mentoring each year.

Talents are a gift from God that can be best realized through service. Each day, think of one way your God-given talents can help someone else. The rewards will be immeasurable!

To each is given the manifestation of the Spirit for the common good. (1 Corinthians 12:7)

Each day, Lord, reveal to me how I can best serve others.

"Things Will Work Out"

Randy Ollis' interest in meteorology dates back to his childhood. Maybe that's why it's not surprising that his faith soars as high as the clouds he loves to study.

That faith wasn't shattered even when his career as a television weather announcer—a lifelong love and passion—was nearly ended by Bell's Palsy.

When the condition inflamed a large nerve in his face, he lost his ability to smile, blink and speak without slurring. It was a nightmare for someone in Randy's profession. Yet, despite everything, Randy always felt that "things would work out."

They did. Although fearful of the public's reaction, his news director let him continue working until he recovered, roughly four months later. The response from viewers was "100 percent positive," with cards and letters to prove it.

What is the touchstone in your life? Upon what foundation have your built your being?

The Lord is my rock, my fortress, and my deliverer...in whom I take refuge. (2 Samuel 22:2,3)

Jesus, You are the rock upon which all of my life, my spirit, my being rests.

Grieving Teens Need You

In the midst of family sadness over a lost loved one, teenagers sometimes get lost in the shuffle.

Matthew recalls that on the day of his grandmother's funeral "nobody looked at me or talked to me. I felt like I was invisible."

Scott was expected to become the man of the family after his father's death. "People were always asking how my mother was doing," he says. They asked about his younger siblings, but, "nobody cared about me!"

Supportive adults can comfort grieving teens by acknowledging their feelings.

Here are a few more ideas:

- be a good listener; respect silences
- allow expression of all kinds of emotions
- send regular notes of encouragement
- give a hug or pat on the back

"Be there" for a grieving teen.

The Lord was my support. (Psalm 18:18)

May I extend my hand to support young people, Lord.

Talking About Values

Parents have many choices to make every day. But, the following thoughts on family life are worth considering:

- It's more important for children to be honorable than on the honor role.
- Instill respect in kids by modeling it.
- Establish consequences for moral lapses.
- Eat meals together—and have conversations.
- Attend worship services together.

Parents cannot teach values without living them. Raising moral children is very time consuming hard work. It requires consistent teaching.

Parents, honor the sacred trust God has placed in you.

The Lord honors a father above his children, and He confirms a mother's right over her children. (Sirach 3:2)

Lord, give parents the strength and courage to do their job well.

Persistence Pays Off

One woman's persistence helped bring about a celebration honoring the 50-year anniversary of the Tuskegee Airmen and the integration of our military to the White House.

The nearly 1,000 Tuskegee Airmen were African-American World War Two fighter pilots at a time when racist attitudes dismissed African-Americans as unable to become pilots. The bravery and effectiveness of the airmen highlighted the wrong-headedness of this view.

Mary Kay Johnson worked as a fund-raiser on a project to restore and use a P51C Mustang fighter plane flown by the Tuskegee Airmen as an educational exhibit. She came to believe that public recognition of the accomplishments of these men was important.

Johnson faced apathy and resistance but prevailed. We too need perseverance to combat injustice. But, it's worth it.

May the God of peace...make you complete in everything good so that you may do His will. (Hebrews 13:20, 21)

God, grant us the courage of our convictions.

A New Waltz

As Rebecca Greer sat at an outdoor skating rink, her hands cupped around a mug of hot chocolate, she noticed a businessman.

After he had pulled a sweater over his suit and began lacing up his skates, Greer couldn't resist asking him how frequently he spent his lunch hour on skates.

"As often as possible," he told her. "It's my therapy. I'm always more efficient afterward."

Greer had never thought of outdoor exercise as therapy before, but decided to change. She began incorporating cross country skiing, hiking, gardening, and swimming into her daily routine. Greer says she always returns to her home office invigorated and ready for work with a clear mind.

"I am enjoying my writing more," she says.

The prophet Miriam, Aaron's sister, took a tambourine in her hand; and all the women went out after her with tambourines and with dancing. (Exodus 15:20)

Teach us new ways to experience life fully, O Lord.

Learning to Love Reading

In her twelve years as an elementary school librarian, Judy Gordon Morrow has learned how to instill a love of reading in children.

- Introduce children to characters they'll love as friends.
- Remember whatever your child's interest, there's a book about it.
- Invite closeness with books.
- Ignite creativity and imagination.
- Inspire compassion, and respect.

Have a book-filled home. Buy books. Go to the library. Spend time reading. Talk about books you enjoy. Take time out to snuggle up in bed with your youngster and a book of their choice.

You'll be raising readers. And bonding with your children.

This book tells the story of Tobit, son of Tobiel son of Hananiel...of the tribe of Naphtali. (Tobit 1:1)

Holy Spirit, may words help me to inspire my children.

That All Might Be Free

Author Jack E. White laments the fact that three decades after the civil rights leader's death, The Rev. Dr. Martin Luther King, Jr.'s achievements remain largely misunderstood.

"He is still regarded mainly as a black leader of a movement for black equality," he wrote in a *Time Magazine* essay. White finds that assessment too limiting. The United States would not be able to claim its role as leader of the "free world" if it weren't for King's movement. "How could the (U.S.) have convincingly inveighed against the Iron Curtain while an equally oppressive Cotton Curtain remained draped across the South?" White asks.

"For all King did to free blacks from the yoke of segregation, whites may owe him the greatest debt for liberating them from the burden of America's centuries-old hypocrisy about race," he concludes.

See Dr. King's words in a new light. -

Look! On the mountains the feet of one who brings good tidings, who proclaims peace! (Nahum 1:15)

Open our hearts to Your message of equality, Lord.

The Doctor Who Dropped In

Dr. Donald Flickinger not only made house calls but he made them by parachute.

Flickinger gained renown during World War II for parachuting into the jungles of Burma (now known as Myanmar). In an area simply marked "unexplored territory" on the map and inhabited by Naga headhunters, he treated downed servicemen and led them to safety.

In August 1943, a transport plane went down on the Chinese border. The 21 crew and passengers, including newsman Eric Sevareid, bailed out; all but one survived. Flickinger and two medics were flown into the area and parachuted to the spot where the survivors were camped. The trade goods Flickinger brought won over the Naga. A month later the entire party emerged from the jungle.

After the war, Dr. Flickinger went on to develop life-support systems for high-altitude flight and space travel, continuing his mission, saving lives.

Honor physicians for their services, for the Lord created them; for their gift of healing comes from the Most High. (Sirach 38:1-2)

Spirit of God, rescue me in times of distress.

A Teacher Learns Forgiveness

For years, teacher Tom Bowers had been obsessed with punishing the man responsible for his sister's death. Bowers' sister Margie had been stabbed to death by Thomas Vanda, the boyfriend of her former roommate, because she had refused to say where her friend had money.

Bowers often asked his father, "Doesn't it make you sick to know that her killer is still alive and Margie's gone?" His father would reply, "There is evil in this world I can't comprehend. I'd rather try to understand the love of God."

One day Bowers was to teach a religion class on forgiveness. He "realized that I could go on hating my sister's murderer, or I could follow Christ's commandment and forgive."

In time, he did forgive. "My father prayed with me, then clasped my hands," Bowers recalls. "I found myself doing what I thought impossible–praying for Thomas Vanda. Words formed in my mind: It's time. Just forgive."

Forgive each other. (Colossians 3:13)

Father, help me to show others Your mercy.

All in a Day's Work?

Back in 1925, Edgar Nollner, who recently died at age 94, figured he was just doing his job.

He was one of 20 "mushers" who, with their 150 dogs, would be hailed as national heroes. The dog sled teams ran in relays through raging Alaskan snowstorms to bring diphtheria antitoxin to a threatened community hundreds of miles away in Nome.

Diphtheria, a highly contagious respiratory ailment, can be fatal. It was imperative that the serum get to the remote area where several cases had been reported. Alaska had only two open-cockpit planes at the time, so winter delivery by air was impractical and dangerous. That's where Nollner and the others came in.

The mushers' fidelity to duty saved lives. Our own devotion on the job may not save lives, but it's of infinite value nonetheless.

The gifts He gave were...to equip the saints for the work of ministry, for building up the body of Christ. (Ephesians 4:11,12)

Jesus, be with us as we go about the day's tasks.

Ten Rules for Business

Combining Gospel principles with sound business practices may be difficult, but it is possible. Archbishop Francois Xavier Nguyn Van Thuan of Vietnam, who is the president of the Pontifical Council for Justice and Peace, makes these suggestions:

1. Be ready. Prepare yourself for your job.
2. Set your goal and resolve to achieve it.
3. Choose trusted collaborators. You can't go it alone.
4. Determine to overcome all obstacles.
5. Make no compromises with corruption.
6. Cultivate good relations.
7. Reserve special attention for children.
8. Be ready to face difficulties and crises.
9. Choose priorities carefully.
10. Train a successor.

Your spiritual beliefs and moral judgments should be part of all you are and do.

Give me the Wisdom that sits by Your throne. (Wisdom of Solomon 9:4)

Spirit of Wisdom, guide my thinking and my decision-making in all aspects of my life.

Translating Faith into Action

As an active member in her church in Lexington, Kentucky, 18-year-old Patricia Valentine was familiar with Jesus' teaching about being "your brother's keeper." When a newborn baby was left in a cardboard box on the steps of her church, Patricia took this teaching to heart.

"He was left at our church," Patricia thought. "That makes him ours." Eager to show her love and concern for the abandoned infant in a special way, Patricia dug through her own baby toys and gave the child her teddy bear and rattle.

The incident encouraged her to organize a community-wide drive to collect stuffed animals for other children in foster care. Thanks to Patricia, the parish donated more than 250.

Caring for others must extend beyond feelings. It's action that brings faith to life.

Just as the body without the spirit is dead, so faith without works is also dead. (James 2:26)

Jesus, no one has ever given a more perfect example of acting on one's beliefs than You. Walk with me so that I may imitate You.

Play Your Way to Youthfulness

Many experts agree that exercise and a high-fiber diet can help you feel good and look younger. But can a good chess match do the same?

According to psychiatrist Gene Cohen, former director of the National Institute of Mental Health's Center on Aging, games are the mental counterpart to physical exertion. He says, "If you work up a mental sweat doing something that's fun, you've tingled your brain cells in a way they won't forget."

To keep brain cells vigorous and the psyche agile, we need to return to the relaxed concentration of childhood.

Why not try a challenging game of bridge, chess or checkers with a friend to invigorate your mind and spirit? Remember, youth is a state of mind as well as of body.

The streets of the city shall be full of boys and girls playing in its streets. (Zechariah 8:5)

Lord, help me view the world with enthusiasm, so I may remain optimistic and positive.

A Little Bit of the Divine

What is that indefinable, ineffable bit of human magic called imagination?

Imagination is not just the power to drift and dream among the clouds (though don't discount that as woolgathering), but serious and difficult work.

Imagination is a point of view created by viewing all points. It is "seeing" things in a different and new way. It puts together talents, quirks, longings and careful calculations into something different.

Gardeners find creative outlets in placing unusual combinations of plants into satisfying arrangements. Musicians take those few notes and create new melodies, much the same way a mother re-cuts a prom dress for another daughter.

All of this is imagination, part of God's creative fun.

Yonder is the sea, great and wide...and Leviathan that you formed to sport in it. (Psalm 104:25,26)

Help me to see Your universe, Lord, with the fresh eyes of a child.

Promises for Parents

Here are some resolutions–for a new year, or a new day–to be better at parenting.

- First things first. Put personal attention before chores and schedules.
- Humor them. Teach your kids to laugh.
- Don't sweat the small stuff. Put yourself in your child's shoes: what means one thing to you may mean something altogether different–or nothing at all–to them.
- "No" is not a four-letter word. Limits are good. Say that out loud, every day.
- Time out. Give your kids space and let them know that sometimes you need it too.
- Give thanks. Say "thank you" to your own parents, for all they did for you.

You can cross your fingers that one day your adult children will be thanking you. Until then, love them today and every day.

When (Jesus') parents saw Him they were astonished. (Luke 2:48)

Father, You love us for who we are and who we can be.

Punishment for Illegal Guns: Exile

"An illegal gun gets you 5 years in Federal Prison."

Billboards, buses, fliers and TV ads with this message have appeared in Richmond, Virginia. The goal: to let "bad guys" know that anytime a gun is found on a drug dealer or user, a convicted felon or a suspect in a violent crime, the case would be tried under tough federal statutes.

Supported by a number of gun-control groups as well as the National Rifle Association, Project Exile has worked. Murders dropped from 140 in 1997 to 94 in 1998. They continue to drop. Close to 300 criminals have gotten long mandatory sentences.

One former drug dealer was afraid to risk prison because he did not want to be separated from his three-year-old son. He got a job in construction, saying, "I straightened up. I couldn't leave him."

Every aspect of life, including law enforcement, gets a boost from creativity. When you face a problem, add a touch of innovation. It might make all the difference.

Knowledge and understanding to...solve problems were found in this Daniel. (Daniel 5:12)

Open my mind and heart to welcome a new Spirit, Holy Lord.

A Boss Learns on the Job

Elaine Pondant thought she'd be a fair, and understanding boss. Yet within months of her promotion to vice-president for a ceiling fan manufacturer, she found herself becoming the kind of boss she'd always abhorred.

One day, Pondant exploded. She called in her staff and told them in no uncertain terms that she was not their mother nor their psychiatrist but their boss, and to leave their problems outside the office.

That evening, she remembered that Jesus told His disciples that to be first of all was to be a servant of all. She realized that her staff looked to her for guidance, advice and sympathy. She went to work the next day determined to set things right.

It so happened it was her birthday, and the same people she had scolded the day before gave her a ceiling fan-shaped card. On each blade were employees' snapshots and birthday messages. With tears running down her cheeks, Pondant said it was "the most wonderful birthday present in the world."

A good boss forgives and asks for forgiveness.

A harsh word stirs up anger. (Proverbs 15:1)

Guide supervisors in relating to their staffs, Carpenter from Nazareth.

The Bible—Poetry and Songs

Sister Joetta Huelsmann, a grade-school teacher in Quincy, Illinois, has discovered an innovative way to introduce the Bible to her students.

Sr. Joetta begins with the Psalms. She explains they are really sacred songs or poems, and the students can create their own to express their relationship with God.

"We talk about King David, who is considered to be the author of the Psalms," she explains. She helps simplify the book by showing students they are generally categorized as songs of sadness, anger or gladness, then encouraging the young people to write their own.

Here is a sample of her young students' work: "Peaceful as a stream flowing into a river, two sea gulls circle the light-blue sky. On the earth, people are rejoicing."

How can you bring God's Word to life for a young person? There's no greater gift you can offer to a young soul than a chance to know God better.

Let the little children come to Me and do not stop them. (Matthew 19:14)

Inspire me with ways to teach young people about you, Jesus.

Progress—And Appreciation

When the World's Fair opened in Queens, New York City, in 1939, crowds were amazed at the display before them, and in particular, at one phenomena, artificial lighting.

In the main theme center, visitors rode a cascading escalator to view a slowly rotating ring-shaped gallery. Encircling a "typical" American city circa 2039 was artificial lighting, symbolizing humankind's progressive march toward the future—hand-in-hand with nature.

Have we lost the ability to be impressed by new inventions or developments? Have we less capacity for appreciating the creativity we see in the technology around us?

You judge by human standards; I judge no one. (John 8:15)

Divine Creator, I thank you for all of the progress we have made in medicine, technology and science. Enable us to make the same progress in eliminating racism, sexism and other forms of intolerance.

Boomer and Gunnar Fight CF

One time NFL star quarterback Boomer Esiason went from the gridiron to a couple of seasons in the TV announcer's booth. Describing his former role as an analyst, he says, "It's probably the only thing in television that remotely comes close to playing quarterback in the NFL."

Esiason is also the founder of the Boomer Esiason Foundation for Cystic Fibrosis (CF) research. His son, Gunnar, has CF. "All we're concerned with is putting enough money into research," says Esiason.

Meanwhile, Gunnar, who receives daily treatment, plays soccer, hockey and baseball, and lives life as fully as possible. Seeing his son thrive and doing all he can to battle CF might be the most rewarding aspect of Esiason's life.

Putting family first is the gratifying way to go.

He who teaches his son will...glory in him among his friends. (Sirach 30:3)

How can I share my assets, time, and talents with members of my own family, Lord Jesus?

Nap Your Way to Serenity

What if your lunch hour at work became two or three hours, during which you went home, ate a leisurely meal, and then nodded off?

An unlikely scenario in the U.S., for certain. Yet in Spain, the tradition of taking a mid-day siesta still prevails for many. Just about everyone who works stops the 'productivity clock' from about one p.m. to roughly four-thirty for lunch with friends and a nap.

This may seem inefficient to us in the States. But the Spanish rank home and social life above work, not the other way around. Science, too, seems to favor the Spanish way: biological research shows that humans' biorhythms naturally crave a midday rest or nap.

What calls the shots in your life? Work? Money? Maybe you really need a time out from the "rat race."

Sweet is the sleep of laborers. (Ecclesiastes 5:12)

Holy Spirit, give me rest from life's activities and stresses.

Jenny Hung GPA 4.43

"Taking honors classes and getting straight A's made me a success. But it didn't make me happy," said Jenny Hung after what she called her "year of sleepless nights."

In an essay for *Newsweek*, Hung describes the freshman year she still remembers with a shudder. Staying up as late as two a.m. became the norm for this driven young woman, who took three honors courses against the better judgment of counselors and friends. She wore sunglasses to school, hiding the dark circles under her eyes.

That May, her name was indeed at the top of a huge list hanging from the ceiling at the school's academic assembly. But her satisfaction was short-lived. "Was that position really important to me?" she wondered.

The next year, Hung chose her classes carefully and incorporated extracurricular activities into her life.

"In the end," she says, "books will fail to teach as much as life itself."

Give your servant therefore an understanding mind...able to discern between good and evil. (1 Kings 3:9)

Is it my will or Yours, O Lord, that is driving my hopes and dreams?

The Soul of the City

When Benedictine Sister Mary Lou Kownacki received an award for her work with the Neighborhood Art House, she quoted humorist Garrison Keillor, "Nothing you do for children is ever wasted...nothing."

Established in an area where all of the families live below poverty, the Art House is an oasis of love.

After school, on weekends, and throughout the summer, hundreds of children receive free lessons in art, poetry, dance, pottery, and music. Volunteers teach and mentor. One local florist visits weekly, bringing armloads of flowers and showing the eager children how to arrange them.

"To see the children running through a blighted neighborhood carrying roses, gladiolas, carnations and even orchids is to understand why we opened the Art House," Kownacki reflected.

One of her colleagues noted that the gift of food and shelter leads to survival; gifts of art, beauty and values lead to a harvest of creativity.

Good sense wins favor. (Proverbs 13:15)

Show us new ways, Father, to feed the hungry.

Answering God's Call—Later in Life

Over the last few decades many men and women have re-evaluated their work and their lives and moved on to something more meaningful. And, in some cases, more spiritual.

More than half of the 65,000 enrolled at Catholic, Protestant and Greek Orthodox seminaries in the U.S. are 35 or older. One-third of those studying to be rabbis or cantors at New York's Jewish Theological Seminary are 30 or older.

Most of these students are willing to risk, to search and to forgo financial rewards for greater spiritual satisfaction. These men and women also feel that God is calling them to serve others.

Audrey Korotkin, 42, a former journalist and marketer, now serves as rabbi of a congregation in Ohio and at several old age homes. Years of study required sacrifice from her family as well as her personal determination, but "it was what my heart was calling me to do."

What is God asking of you?

Let yourselves be built into a spiritual house, to be a holy priesthood. (1 Peter 2:5)

Help me know Your will, Lord, and help me live it.

Technology Is Not Neutral

If you think that technologies are problems only if you lack access to them, think again.

Historian Daniel Boorstin says, "technology insulates and isolates," invents its own needs and creates its own momentum.

A study from Carnegie Mellon University's Human Computer Interaction Institute, notes that Internet use decreases psychological well-being, "building shallow relationships," and a "decline in feelings of connection to other people."

Technology is a tool. Quicker does not necessarily mean better, nor does knowledge equal wisdom. We must use our own judgment.

Arnold Toynbee commented: "Everyone now alive has been charged with a sacred trust. The making of choices is a heavy burden for us human beings; but our power to choose and to decide is an open door for hope. This God-given power is our distinctive human characteristic."

Choose life...loving the Lord...obeying Him, and holding fast to Him. (Deuteronomy 30:19,20)

Spirit of Wisdom, show me Your way and Your will.

When Trust Doesn't Come Easily

Marvel Castro of Syracuse, New York finally heard the words she'd only heard in dreams. "Mrs. Castro, we have a kidney for you."

However, with no family nearby and limited finances, she would have to entrust her two children to a local social services agency during her recovery. How could she trust someone else to take care of those who mattered most to her in the world?

Mrs. Castro asked God to send someone to take care of her babies. Debbi Hier, a mother of two children, agreed to care for Marvel's kids while she recovered. When Marvel finally met Debbi, she realized that this was a friend God had sent to comfort and love her and her children when they needed it most.

Trusting others is especially difficult when we are vulnerable. Yet it is precisely when we're vulnerable that we can experience trusting others fully for the first time.

Trust in the Lord. (Proverbs 3:5)

Father God, enable me to trust Your endless, boundless love for me.

Talented, Creative and Homeless

Why would someone who is having a hard time getting food, clothing and shelter care about the arts?

For people who are overwhelmed by life on the streets, frustrated by bureaucratic red tape and possibly dealing with mental health issues, the arts provide a tangible plus. Several New York neighborhood groups encourage homeless men and women to express themselves through writing, painting and photography.

For a few hours a week, they connect with a larger world while using their God-given talents. Pam Parlapiano, a photography teacher at Pathways to Housing, says that "they have incredibly unharnessed creativity. I'm just giving them a chance to see it. ...It's one step further into society."

Everybody needs a sense of self-worth and belonging. Each day encourage those in need to do something positive for themselves.

Love the Lord your God with all your heart, and with all your soul, and with all your mind...love your neighbor as yourself. (Matthew 22:37,39)

Jesus, don't let me neglect my neighbors' needs for life's essentials.

For the Greater Good

Why does altruism seems to come so easily to some? Probably because of the way their parents raised them.

"Telling your kids to be altruistic is not enough," says University of Wisconsin sociologist Jane Piliavan. "Adults who volunteer...report that their parents were volunteers."

We can develop a more altruistic outlook. Imagine what it is like to be in another person's shoes. Reject stereotypes. Learn to be tolerant of people who are "different." Value justice not only for yourself but for all. Be generous. Have confidence in your ability to create change.

And nurture a "spirituality that believes we all belong to the human family...that everyone is part of a common universe," says sociologist Samuel Oliner of California's Humboldt State University.

It is not lip service to call ourselves children of God. It is the truth.

Train children in the right way, and when old, they will not stray. (Proverbs 22:6)

Dear Father, bless us, Your children.

God, Why Don't You Answer?

"Don't you see what's happening?" Clifford Sigler demanded of God. "Why don't you help?"

The middle-aged ex-Marine and divorced father was in despair at the mess he'd made of his life. Yet he clung to a sliver of hope.

Sigler had spent years "crippled by drinking and drugging." He'd left his wife and abandoned his three children. One day he heard God answer with a challenge to help others.

Sigler decided to clean up his act and work against drug sellers. Local law enforcement gave him enough work to keep him busy and fulfilled.

The real reward came when his grown daughter asked him to be in her wedding. Reconciliation with his wife followed. Sigler asked for forgiveness and learned to forgive himself.

You are holy, enthroned on the praises of Israel. In You our ancestors trusted...and You delivered them. (Psalm 22:3-4)

Help us mend our ways and broken relationships, Lord.

Have Faith in Your Dreams

When Michele Gonada graduated from Penn State in 1984, her degree in microbiology led to several jobs with pharmaceutical companies. Within five years she had patented one of the first "quick response" tests for AIDS.

"I felt good about my accomplishments," she says, but they didn't satisfy her creative spirit.

Then she was transferred to Los Angeles. An invitation to a friend's bridal shower changed her life. "It was held in a designer's showroom," Gonda explained, "and I knew that I was in the right place."

Within a week Gonda left her test tubes to work in the clothing industry. Soon she was designing and today, her firm sells to chains. Her company, Faith Couture, is named for the huge leap of faith she took in following her dream. And her designs often show up in fashion shows that benefit charities.

What is your dream?

Whoever serves must do so with the strength that God supplies, so that God may be glorified in all things through Jesus Christ. (1 Peter 4:11)

Give us faith to follow Your path, Lord.

The Mystery of Sleep

We do it every night, or try to. But how much do we really know about sleep? In some ways it remains a mystery, even to scientists.

Here are a few interesting tidbits about sleep from American Demographics:

- Percent of men who snore: 36
- Percent of women who snore: 23
- Percent who sleep with two pillows: 42.6
- Percent who sleep with none: 3.2
- Percent who consider sleep a necessity: 66
- Percent who always get a restful night's sleep: 25
- Average daily hours of sleep for us: 7.5
- Average daily hours of sleep for our cats: 15

Various theories have been proposed and debunked about what sleep is and why we need it. Whatever sleep's purpose, one bout of insomnia is convincing personal evidence of its value.

I will both lie down and sleep in peace; for you alone, O Lord, make me lie down in safety. (Psalm 4:8)

Lord, may we all know the bliss of a good night's sleep.

The Simple Truth

"I think one person can make a difference," said Doug Wylie, a railroad engineer with Norfolk Southern Corporation. Wylie was awarded the Harold F. Hammond Award for outstanding achievement in safety.

The company makes the safety of employees and the public a top priority. One way in which the message is frequently underscored is by reminding workers how important they are to their families and their co-workers.

Wylie accepted the national award with praise for his colleague, conductor Jack Pettyjohn. "I've learned from Jack that we are our brothers' and sisters' keepers," he commented.

Wylie also shared a simple nugget of wisdom which bears repeating: "count your blessings, you will look at life entirely differently."

When was the last time you truly expressed your gratitude for the many blessings in your life?

With gratitude in your hearts sing psalms, hymns and spiritual songs to God. (Colossians 3:16)

Giver of Life, may we cherish each other as You cherish us.

Lessons for School on the Web

When Sue McNutt, a mother of two in Omaha, Nebraska, heard her public school system was gaining access to the Internet, she asked for the opportunity to help them write a policy that would block student access to pornography by using filtering programs.

Instead, a policy was proposed that included no filters. "When God is in your life, you want to make a difference," McNutt says, and so she fought back. After almost two years and many meetings and telephone calls, she was able to stop the policy from being adopted. In fact, she wrote her own policy which was unanimously accepted by the Omaha school board.

"My ultimate goal would be for all schools to filter the Internet," McNutt says. "But you... learn not to give up, because the cause is right–and God is there with you."

Her advice to parents: "Be informed–and make sure you have prayer support" in this struggle.

Wisdom gives life to the one who possesses it. (Ecclesiastes 7:12)

Give me the courage of my convictions, Lord.

Truly Best Friends

Jazz and Ranger are fearless. They work at a moment's notice, in snow and rain, on rivers, and in rubble. They're dedicated dogs, trained for search and rescue missions.

While their volunteer handlers commonly refer to themselves as "the stupid part of the team," in truth they are also highly-skilled. They must learn to read even the subtlest signs in their dogs.

And the teams must be ready to go anywhere at a moment's notice, usually in less-than-ideal conditions.

In order to stay at peak condition, the teams train up to 1000 hours each year. The trainers' reward? "There's nothing better than a live find," says Marcia Koenig. She and her dog, Coyote, were once called into a search 18 hours after it began. Coyote took less than ten minutes to find the victim, dazed but very much alive.

As for the dogs, exuberant praise and a rough and tumble game of frisbee is enough.

The greatest among you will be your servant. (Matthew 23:11)

Give us attitudes of servanthood, Lord, ready to serve others at a moment's notice.

A Woman's Voice for Equality

Barbara Jordan had the distinction of being the first woman and only black woman elected to the Texas Senate...in Texas' Congressional delegation...from the South. The degree of prejudice she had to overcome by her intelligence and sheer force of personality is impossible to overestimate.

She was a magna cum laude graduate of Texas Southern University, earned her law degree from Boston University, won election to the Texas Senate, and saw to the establishment of Texas' first black Congressional district.

Barbara Jordan defined public service as a commitment to using government to help achieve liberty and justice for everyone. And she inspired women and people of color to prepare themselves for such a life in public service through education.

Senator Jordan said that her "faith in the Constitution is whole, it is complete, it is total."

How total is your faith in the Constitution? How do you live that faith?

Hate evil...establish justice. (Amos 5:15)

We as a nation are prejudiced and judgmental, Father. Forgive us these sins against You and our sisters and brothers, Your children.

Are you Ready?

The wealth of book titles, newsletters, and web sites dedicated to simplicity suggest people are more than tired of the chaotic treadmill of life. *Family Circle* published a short quiz to help readers determine if they might be ready to simplify: "Do you come home from work exhausted?"; are you "in debt? overwhelmed by clutter? Have little time for family, friends, self?"

Author Sherry Cohen encourages readers to begin by establishing their own definition of success. She points to Debbie Ford's *The Dark Side of the Light Chasers: Reclaiming Your Power, Creativity, Brilliance, and Dreams.*

"Instead of focusing on your weaknesses or on other people's dreams," Ford writes, "recognize where your power lies. Decide what's important and worthy...then establish your own agenda."

What or who guides your decisions?

Learn where there is wisdom...strength...understanding...length of days and life...peace. ...She is the book of the commandments of God, the law that endures forever. (Baruch 3:14, 4:1)

Help us clean out the clutter in our minds, Father, so we can find You more readily.

Graceful Hearts

When thirty-eight-year-old Elizabeth Ann Bartlett, an associate professor of political science at the University of Minnesota, and a vibrant wife and mother was stricken with heart problems, she was devastated.

Consumed with resentment at all she had lost, including hopes for a long and carefree life with her family, she realized she would need to find the blessings in her illness to survive.

"As the...tenuousness of my life sank in, I came to see each day as a gift," she says. She discovered an interweaving of grace and gratitude, and found that a daily appreciation of the ordinary gifts grants us grace.

Bartlett has since received a new heart through a successful transplant operation. "I think the real gift I received in receiving the new heart is the gift of knowing gratitude in such a deep and profound way." She reflects, "Little did I know how much receiving a new physical heart would also transform my spiritual heart."

"Come," my heart says, "seek His face!" Your face, Lord, do I seek. (Psalm 27:8)

Lord, give us hearts that celebrate the wonder of ordinary days.

Artist Encourages Youngsters

"I encourage everyone to become their dream," says James De La Vega.

A native of New York's Spanish Harlem, the muralist and painter has become known citywide for his sidewalk art. But he has not forgotten his roots. He teaches art to youngsters just as he started to take lessons shortly after he got his first box of crayons.

De La Vega is also a motivational speaker. "Most young people get sidetracked and never do what they really set out to do. Life becomes more of a game of survival and they have to work to put food on their table. "There is nothing wrong with that, but I encourage people not to lose sight of what they want to do. If they cannot afford to do it full time, I tell them to do it as a hobby."

It is oh-so-easy to see early dreams sidetracked. That's a shame. God does not want us to waste our talents. Instead, put your precious gifts to use now.

There are varieties of gifts, but the same Spirit. (1 Corinthians 12:4)

Son of God, You want me to use Your gifts. Help me appreciate and rejoice in them.

Food from Above

In the Old Testament, God provided for His people in extraordinary ways. We call them miracles. When He inspires others to use their common sense, we don't call it a miracle, we call it caring. But, whenever a human heart is touched with compassion, in today's hectic and self-centered world, we could call it a miracle.

A program sponsored by American Airlines donates unopened, unused airline food to local food banks. Comedians put down airline food. But for some, this food is highly desirable and much needed. So over 10,000 pounds of sealed, nonperishable food has been donated to local food banks in Dallas. The idea is spreading to other cities.

As Dee Dee Caidin, an American flight attendant said, "This is something we saw a need for and pursued. ...It's all real high quality."

Caring and sharing are wise decisions for corporations and individuals alike.

A generous person will be enriched.
(Proverbs 11:25)

Teach me, dear God, the value of thrift, the glory of sharing.

A Word from Wise

Multi-tasking is one of those nineties buzz-words that sounds like a solution. Think of all the time that you could save if only you consistently did more than one thing at a time!

Author Nicole Wise advises against this fallacy, especially when it comes to parenting. "If you're simultaneously spooning yogurt into your child's mouth, talking on the phone, and watching your preschooler color," she points out, "you're actually experiencing, and enjoying, little of it."

Wise believes a more peaceful existence is possible by "being fully and passionately involved in your life, even in the daily minutiae like folding laundry (inhaling the freshness and feeling the warmth of the clean clothes)."

There are occasions when it's necessary, even sensible to do more than one thing at a time. But a willingness to slow down and focus can bring richness to scattered moments throughout each day.

**For everything there is a season.
(Ecclesiastes 3:1)**

Reveal Yurself to us, O Lord, in places we haven't looked before.

Tuning Out—or In?

For proper brain development, babies need close-up interaction with people.

So...turn off the television. The American Academy of Pediatrics suggests no television for children under 2 years of age; supervised viewing thereafter.

Defending its "no TV" ruling, the Academy says that if babies are watching television, they are not getting the needed human stimuli for intellectual development. Many parents agree but stop at setting limits unless a child shows social, emotional or other developmental problems.

The Academy, for its part, cites studies linking violence in movies and television to aggressive behavior in young people.

"It's not a bad thing for health professionals to remind parents that they need to be aware of the risks (of television)," says Robert Lichter, president of the Center for Media and Public Affairs, a nonprofit research group in Washington, D.C.

What's best? Tune in to your children.

Get wisdom; get insight. (Proverbs 4:5)

Keep watch over my children this day, Lord. Guide them.

Resting Place at Gettysburg

More than 40,000 soldiers died in the July, 1863 Gettysburg, Pennsylvania, Civil War battle.

When the carnage was over, the battleground became our first national cemetery. President Abraham Lincoln's address at the dedication contained these memorable lines:

"Four score and seven years ago our fathers brought forth on this continent a new nation, conceived in liberty and dedicated to the proposition that all men are created equal. ...we here highly resolve that these dead shall not have died in vain; that this nation, under God, shall have a new birth of freedom, and that government of the people, by the people, for the people shall not perish from the earth."

The press criticized him for a speech that was too mild and too brief. We know Lincoln's Gettysburg Address as a remarkable statement of resolve to keep a nation growing according to the vision of its founders. We still have parts to play in our nation's growth.

Bring good news to the oppressed...proclaim liberty to the captives, and release to the prisoners. (Isaiah 61:1)

Share with me, Holy Spirit, Your own courage to follow You in all things.

All Good Gifts

"I try to recall the last real present she gave me, but I can't," says Angela Haight of her mother, whose memory and behavior are suffering the ravages of aging.

On a trip home from seeing a play, Haight's mother remarked about the "lovely symphony" they had just attended. Her mother's comment reminded her that she came to love the symphony through her mother's persistence in taking her to the Saturday morning children's concerts.

"Haight remembers other "gifts:" summer afternoons when her mother would read stories to her and her friends; weekly trips to the library; armfuls of books she helped her carry home.

"No matter how much my mother's condition deteriorates," Haight notes, "her gifts are…mine as long as I live–and longer as I pass them on to my own children and grandchildren."

Those who respect their mother are like those who lay up treasure. (Sirach 3:4)

Master, enable us today, to serve You by bringing Your love to others.

A Joyful Man

For 46 years Sam Cohen sliced lox at Zabar's, a store on Manhattan's Upper West Side. But he did more than cut and wrap salted, smoked salmon. According to his obituary in *The New York Times*, he created "a joyous life behind the counter after a sorrowful past in which he barely escaped the Holocaust and lost most of his family."

Sam Cohen grew up in Poland and was a businessman before the Second World War. He escaped from a concentration camp and, in 1952, came to New York. Not long afterwards he found his niche. With an ability to speak Polish, English, Hebrew, Russian, and Spanish, he served customers with humor and charm. He put his daughter through dental school and his son through medical school by working 60 hours a week.

A co-worker called him "the most joyful" man he had ever known. A customer who had come to America in the same ship as Sam Cohen said that "all he cared about was doing the best he could." What better legacy could anyone leave?

A joyful heart is life itself, and rejoicing lengthens one's life span. (Sirach 30:22)

Spirit of Courage, inspire me to embrace life despite pain and to share my best with all I meet.

Kids Just Want to be Kids

No doubt parents have more to worry about than ever before, right? There's no shortage of anxieties to fixate on–the corrupting influences of certain aspects of popular culture and advertising, random school violence.

Still, according to a Nickelodeon and *Time* poll, kids don't view the world as the dangerous place their parents do.

Asked whom they admire most, 79% said mom and dad; an additional 19% their grandparents. God plays a large part. 95% said they were believers; 8 out of 10 say they pray. 76% of those 12 to 14 say it's important to delay sex until marriage.

Are parents worrying for no reason? Could it be that the great majority of kids are alright? The good news is, that kids are happy to be kids–playing, hanging with friends and having fun–and are in no hurry to grow up.

Sometimes, the more things change the more they remain the same.

What has been is what will be...there is nothing new under the sun. (Ecclesiastes 1:9)

Watch over and protect children, Father.

Feel Good by Doing Good

"Volunteering...makes you feel good about yourself, and it makes you optimistic about the world and about humanity," says realtor and mother Margaret Romero of Taos, New Mexico.

Romero volunteers her free hour or so each week to the committee that recommends families for Habitat for Humanity home ownership. She reviews applications, interviews families, and visits their home.

Marilyn Thomas is also a volunteer. She always wanted to work in a museum. When she and her husband retired, she designed a docent, or tour guide, program at the Museum of Northern New Mexico. In return she has learned about Native American and Hispanic art and culture through museum events. She says that volunteering offers fulfillment even as it "broadens your experience" and gives "the chance to make a difference."

How can you make a difference by being generous with your time and talents?

Serve one another with whatever gift each of you has received. (1 Peter 4:10)

Jesus, inspire my generosity with time, talents and interests.

What's Fun Got to Do With It?

Consider this disheartening trend in the once-light hearted world of children's Little League: some children are feeling such pressure to "be the best" in their leagues that parents have hired professional tutors to help boost their kids' batting averages! Often, this "extra help" is available at $70 an hour and up.

In an article in the *The New York Times*, many parents admitted their children are stressed out from the pressure to succeed not only in academics, but also in the extra-curricular activities that used to be fun. Many of these overstressed children are barely 10-years-old.

Success is a subjective thing. How successful is a life without fun, joy, leisure? Parents can impart this idea to their children.

We beseech You, give us success! (Psalm 118:25)

Jesus, You taught us that the Kingdom of Heaven is one of joy, not worry and anxiety. I pray for the mindfulness to enjoy life whenever possible.

Thanks for the Little Push

One of syndicated columnist Dear Abby's fans waited nearly a decade to thank her for a letter Abby had published.

The reader wanted to return to school to become a teacher, but was concerned because she would be 40 upon graduation. "Then I read a letter in your column about someone in a similar situation," the reader wrote. "After thinking about your answer to that question, I decided to enroll."

In response, Abby reprinted the original letter, which had been written by a 36-year-old college dropout who had always wanted to be a physician. The reader, who had a good job with a pharmaceutical company, was hesitating about returning to college and applying to medical school because it would take seven years before he could practice medicine. "I will be 43 years old," he wrote. "What do you think?"

Abby answered with a simple question. "And how old will you be in seven years if you don't go to medical school?"

Do not worry about tomorrow...Today's trouble is enough for today. (Matthew 6:34)

Show us the folly of our fears, Loving Father.

I Know Just How You Feel!

Roberta Israeloff thinks listening is becoming a lost art.

She has noticed that in the name of empathy, people often turn conversations around, launching into their own stories. Although the intention may be good, people often say, "I know just how you feel and I can prove it." Or maybe even top it.

Israeloff has made a conscious effort to stop interrupting her friends.

"I've come to think of it as a dance in which I'm learning to follow the other person's lead," she says, "to pay attention to body language, facial gestures, tone of voice; to hear what's left unsaid; to recall relevant details and make helpful associations and connections."

Share your own experiences, but use them to illuminate your friends' situations, not overshadow them, Israeloff says. She calls this ability "the cornerstone of genuine empathy."

Listen carefully to my words. (Job 13:17)

Help me to step aside, Lord, and open my ears and heart to hear others completely.

The First Lady of Song

Did you know that Ella Fitzgerald, who practically invented "scat" singing and helped establish the popular standard as an art form, suffered greatly throughout her life? Yet despair had no place in her musical styling; she instead opted for harmony and swing.

Abused by a stepfather after her mother died, Fitzgerald became a teenage truant who did time in a state reformatory. She ran away to the streets of Harlem, singing and dancing for small change, and eventually won singing contests at places like the Apollo Theater. She lacked glamour, and big band leaders were hesitant to hire her. Radio and records brought her voice and talent the prominence she merited. She performed into the 1990's, despite the onslaught of diabetes that deprived her of her eyesight, both legs and, finally, her life.

Ella Fitzgerald suffered but her musicality was a balm for her pain. She was the real deal, an example never to sing or even speak in any voice other than the one that is your own.

Sing and make melody. (Psalm 57:7)

I will sing a song of life and love, Lord Jesus.

Using the Thumb Prayer

Do you know the Thumb Prayer?

Page McKean Zyromski not only knows it - it seems as if she and her six-year-old daughter created it. One evening at bedtime, the little girl was too tired to say her prayers and asked, "Can I just do the thumb prayer?"

At first, Zyromski was perplexed. What is the thumb prayer, she wondered. But she quickly recalled having taught her daughter that gestures as well as words can be prayers. "I pointed out that it's a prayer all by itself when we make a little cross with our thumb on the forehead, lips, and heart before the Gospel at Mass."

Then one day when the six year old was fidgety in church, her mother suggested saying their Thumb Prayer. Tracing a little cross on her palm helped her daughter settle herself down.

Zyromski suggests the little prayer gesture can be used while waiting on grocery lines; when you're having trouble sleeping; or even to calm and center oneself during emotional upset.

Prayer doesn't have to entail spoken words. Sometimes a little gesture can go a long way.

**Pray to your Father who is in secret.
(Matthew 6:6)**

Jesus, teach us how to pray.

Astounding Info

There's nothing necessarily wrong with having money, using cosmetics, eating ice cream, buying pet food, or having, buying, or enjoying any of the other good things of life.

But, the world's 225 richest people have assets of $1 trillion plus. This equals the annual income of the world's poorest 47%. Here are some economic realities from the United Nations Human Development Report.

People in the U.S. spend about $8 billion on cosmetics when that sum could give everyone a basic education—with $2 billion left over. Europeans spend $11 billion on ice cream, yearly. That would more than pay for water and sewer systems for all the world's people. The $17 billion spent for pet food in the U.S. and Europe would buy basic nutrition and health care for the world's people—with $4 billion left.

What *is* wrong is our not recognizing and meeting the challenge to use some money we put toward "the good life" so that others may also have a more fully human life.

Open your hand to the poor and needy neighbor in your land. (Deuteronomy 15:11)

You've given me all I have and enjoy, Generous Lord. May careful stewardship be an expression of my gratitude.

Taming Anger

Are there any ways to prevent stress and anger before they start? Here are some ideas.

- Accept conflict as normal in relationships.
- Disagree without being disagreeable. Don't insist that everyone agree with you.
- Know that the obvious source of the conflict isn't always the real rub.
- Remember that sometimes conflict is used to attract attention.
- Be responsible for how you feel and for what happens to you.
- Be patient and forgiving. Most people are doing their best

None of these ideas mean you should let someone take advantage of you. But patience goes a long way toward preventing anger.

Live in harmony with one another...do not repay anyone evil for evil...live peaceably with all. (Romans 12:16,17,18)

Jesus, help me accept anger as a normal, human emotion, neither good nor bad—until we make it so.

The Power of Prayer

Prayer is more than a form of expression or meditation. Prayer is communication with the Living God, who is listening and responding to your voice.

Only with God's help and only with prayer can some mountains be moved. Only through prayer do we have the strength to work, to live the lives that God wants for us.

Brother Lawrence, author of the *Practice of the Presence of God*, wrote "It is a great delusion to think that times of prayer are different from other times.

How often do you pray? Try praying consistently, every day, and if possible, at about the same time. Incorporate prayer into your daily life.

In the morning, while it was still very dark, [Jesus] got up and went out to a deserted place, and there He prayed. (Mark 1:35)

Restore calm to my soul and rejuvenate my spirit by teaching me to pray, Holy Spirit.

Illuminating the Bible Letter by Letter

For the first time in the five hundred years since printing presses replaced handwritten manuscripts, a bible is being created one letter at a time.

St. John's Abbey and St. John's University of Collegeville, Minnesota, have commissioned Donald Jackson, a renowned calligrapher, to consult with artists, theologians and scribes to produce a new Bible. It is scheduled to be complete by 2004. Using parchment and written with quill pens, the Bible will incorporate traditional as well as modern religious and cultural influences.

Brother Dietrich Reinhart, the Benedictine president of the University, says the aim is "to ignite the imagination of the world with a remarkable contemporary work of art, and to illuminate God's Word by reviving an ancient monastic tradition."

Open your Bible. Take a new look at the Word of God. Read it aloud. Write out a few verses for yourself. Pray the Bible daily.

All scripture is inspired by God and is useful for teaching, for reproof, for correction, and for training in righteousness so that everyone who belongs to God may be proficient, equipped for every good work. (2 Timothy 3:16)

Paraclete, open my heart and mind to Your Word.

I Am Beautiful

In 1997 Dana Carpenter and Woody Winfree wrote a book, *I Am Beautiful: A Celebration of Women in Their Own Words.* The essays they composed along with stunning black and white photos of their subjects, have helped to give both men and women a new perspective on the meaning of beauty.

Women dealing with adversity and finding strength and confidence despite circumstances that might dictate otherwise, show the way when they proudly proclaim "I am beautiful."

The book has spawned a documentary film and intergenerational workshops are springing up around the country. Teenagers struggling to find their identity, mothers seeking to impart healthy self-esteem to their children, and women who proudly bear life's scars are coming together to celebrate their goodness.

If you were going to be part of such a project, what thoughts might you share about your own beauty?

[Judith] was beautiful in appearance and very lovely to behold...No one spoke ill of her, for she feared God with great devotion. (Judith 8:7,8)

Open our eyes to the miraculous beauty You have created in each of us, Lord.

The Facts about Fibbing

Most of us consider ourselves to be honest and truthful people, correct? Truth be told, it's not easy to keep from telling a fib, or fibs, almost daily.

Think of the Jim Carrey comedy, *Liar, Liar,* in which he plays a lawyer whose son makes a birthday wish that his dad will not tell a lie for 24 hours. According to a study by University of Virginia psychologist Bella DePaulo, most Americans lie nearly as often as they brush their teeth.

- Ever called in sick to the office, or told the boss your ill children needed you at home—and you're paid for the day to boot?
- Ever told an anxious friend that a new hairdo looks good, when you think just the opposite?
- Ever lied about the number of cookies in a cookie jar to a whining child?

Food for thought, eh? To become more honest in everyday life means being honest in one situation after another, and choosing to do so over and over again. It's a challenge to live more honestly.

Birds roost with their own kind, so honesty comes home to those who practice it. (Sirach 27:9)

Guide me to live with daily integrity in my heart, Holy Spirit.

Life Coaching

Feeling unfulfilled in your career? Not having enough fun in your life? Losing sight of individual aspirations and feeling overwhelmed by family obligations? Perhaps you could benefit from some coaching.

Personal coaching has become a trend. A combination of friend, mentor and therapist, a coach can encourage, brainstorm with, and prod a client about goals and values. Besides helping with their professional lives, coaches encourage people to look at relationships, recreational pursuits, and even spirituality.

"Coaching tends to look forward," says one coach, Christine Johnson D'Amico. "It's about spending time looking at who you are and how you want to be."

There is a downside to this new trend: it is possible to become more self-absorbed, more selfish about individual needs and time. As always, balance is the key.

A coach can be helpful in determining goals, desires, and priorities. Ultimately however, it's up to each one of us to pray and to then make decisions.

By prayer and supplication with thanksgiving let your requests be made known to God. (Philippians 4:6)

God, the ultimate Coach, guide me.

The Image Collector

Otto L. Bettman was a pack rat with a vision. When he left Germany in 1935 – Jews were still allowed to emigrate – he took with him to America two large trunks filled with, well, junk. Or so he thought. Those piles of photographs and copied images would become the foundation of an archive that came to be worth millions.

The son of a bibliophile, Bettman became a curator of rare books and an aficionado of imagery through the ages. He had a scholar's sense of history and an artist's eye. Today, the archive he began is comprised of 16 million images and is owned by Bill Gates.

We often poke fun at those who hoard and hide away ticket stubs, newspaper clippings, photos, posters and the like. Yet it may well be that the future belongs to those who save and collect keepsakes. It's only by reviewing our past that we can move forward with knowledge and insight.

(God) has made everything suitable for its time; moreover He has put a sense of past and future into their minds. (Ecclesiastes 3:11)

I cherish what has gone before me, Lord. Help me learn from it.

After the Fall

One minute Paula Jean Nichols-Klimin was a successful model, the next she was plummeting 10 stories in an out-of-control elevator cab. When she woke up in the hospital, she couldn't move her legs. Today, her right leg remains paralyzed.

At first, Nichols-Klimin was emotionally traumatized and in constant pain. For two years, she hardly ever left her apartment except for physical therapy sessions. She had gained weight and couldn't reconcile her new size with her old, razor-thin self. "After much soul-searching, I gradually came to like the new me," she says.

Eventually, too, she met Victor Klimin and they married. She has even set up a school for aspiring performers and models; classes include disabled students.

Nichols-Klimin admits that there are days when she asks, "Why me?" She wonders what her life would have been had she never gotten on that elevator. "But I find strength in prayer," she says—and in the notes of those who write to tell her that her example has made a difference for them.

I can do all things through Him who strengthens me. (Philippians 4:12)

When I am lost, Master, show me the way.

Overcoming Being Perfect

June does everything perfectly – exactly right. Throughout the years, her sense of perfection gradually became a prison.

Too many people today suffer within the confining walls of perfectionism, aiming to please God but ending up self-righteous, exacting and fearfully scrupulous.

The following hints may help those in "perfect prison" find release:

- God doesn't demand perfection. Jesus, in fact, was criticized because He ate with sinners.

- Meditation on Jesus' gracious acceptance and kindness toward all can help you break free.

- Let go of anger. Anger over others' actions or words, held tight inside and not released, can suffocate you and shut off your energy for positive, life-giving activity.

- Channel energies into helping others.

A chat with Jesus is always helpful. There's nothing wrong with taking a moment to pray: "God I'm not perfect. Help me to love myself 'as is'.

[Jesus] said..."I have come to call not the righteous but sinners." (Mark 2:17)

Your words, Jesus, comfort me.

A Wonderful Determination

At age 11, a young North Dakotan suffered a ruptured appendix. After surgery, he began playing musical instruments to entertain himself until he could return to work on the farm.

Years later, he left to seek his fortune in the music industry. He never considered giving up even though he struggled to make a living. When money was tight, he and his wife raised chickens on the side. Moving from city to city, he learned everything he could about leading a band. Eventually, he became the band's announcer and his charm appealed to audiences around the country.

Finally, in 1955, 31 years after leaving the farm, Lawrence Welk made his television debut with his Champagne Orchestra. For decades more, he entertained audiences, earning the immense popularity that had so long eluded him.

Achievement usually demands a high price. It's called persistence.

Bear fruit with patient endurance. (Luke 8:15)

Keep us faithful to the song you put in each of our hearts, dear Lord.

Build It and They Will Eat

Twenty years ago no one suspected that the Jubilee Kitchen in the Hill District of Pittsburgh would still be feeding the needy today. The kitchen serves hot lunches to 150 people a day.

Liguori Rossner and Joyce Rothermel began the soup kitchen in 1979 with just $9.36. Unions sent apprentice carpenters, plumbers, tile setters. Companies contributed goods and architects their services.

Job training has been added. Used clothing is available. And soon they'll begin a day care center for 20 children of working mothers.

Jubilee Kitchen is an ecumenical project helped by local houses of worship: Protestant, Catholic and Jewish. Volunteers who come to serve say: "What draws you in is the people in need."

The dream of two women twenty years ago continues to be a light in the darkness.

Just as you did it to one of the least of these who are members of My family, you did it to Me. (Matthew 25:40)

Create in me a wellspring of compassion and concern, Jesus.

Ambassador of Hope

When social worker Nadine Goodman first arrived in Mexico in 1981, she intended to study Spanish to better serve the Puerto Ricans living in New York.

Instead, she married a Mexican man, and stayed.

Her life's surprises didn't end there—Goodman decided to continue her social work in Mexico.

She developed a one-woman family health project in Central Mexico into an internationally recognized outreach and health care agency. More than 50,000 people are served each year. Women and children are empowered through information on domestic violence, AIDS, alcoholism, even ecology.

It is possible for people to make a difference for the better wherever they are. What can you do?

Help the weak, be patient with all.
(1 Thessalonians 5:14)

Lord, Your disciples were Your ambassadors. Give me the character and courage to follow their example bringing hope to even one person.

Surgeon Offers Hope

Milton Waner is a plastic and reconstructive surgeon at Arkansas Children's Hospital in Little Rock. To many, he's also a miracle worker.

Dr. Waner repairs the disfigured faces of those with growths called hemangiomas and vascular malformations. Vascular birthmarks are a medical concern and also a psychological one.

The parents of a boy with a large lesion on his upper lip worried that he might hurt himself and bleed uncontrollably. It was also obvious that the youngster's twin received positive attention from strangers while his brother drew stares.

After Dr. Waner's corrective surgery, the boy "has started trying to kiss us," according to his father, "something he never did before."

For his part, the surgeon says, "Every time, I operate as if it were my child, and I have to do more than my best."

Give the physician his place, for the Lord created him. (Sirach 38:12)

Lord, give us wise and caring doctors.

You Can't Choose Your Family

Reunions are gaining in popularity. They are now estimated at about 200,000 a year across the United States.

There are few things as daunting as looking out over a field and seeing it filled with those who are related to you. And just what is the difference between a first cousin once removed and a second cousin?

Be assured that those you haven't seen in years will remember you just as you were and are not afraid to say things like: "My, your skin has cleared up nicely!" And everyone will be compared to people who died decades ago.

Still, reunions offer us the chance to connect with our roots, with a history which is as rich and varied as creation itself. They offer a wonderful reminder that we are participants in the ongoing story of our family.

Among family members their leader is worthy of honor. (Sirach 10:20)

Thank You, Lord, for my family, for my friends, and for the opportunity to love.

Old Age: Definitely Not For Sissies

The fastest growing segment of the population in the United States is the 85 plus age group.

Modern medicine has raised the possibility that most of us could live to be well over 100. In order to achieve this milestone, though, certain things are important, not the least of which is staying healthy throughout one's life.

In a recent survey sponsored by the American Association of Retired Persons, some were exhilarated at the prospect of a long life. But 62% said they did not want to live to such an advanced age. They cited worries over health, lack of money, loss of mental facilities, dependence upon others, becoming a burden, becoming isolated, or living in a nursing home.

We need to remember that it is God who gives and sustains life. It is up to us to live life well, the way God envisioned for us from the very beginning, healthily, joyfully.

The days of our life are seventy years or perhaps eighty, if we are strong. (Psalm 90:10)

Give me length of days, O Lord, to glorify Your Name.

Prayer—With Others in Mind

Perhaps you've heard one or two of the many versions of "An Irish Blessing." Perhaps too, its original meaning has been taken for granted.

Yet, the poem, no matter which version, focuses on a single wish: a deep and sincere blessing on the listener or reader. An interesting thought—since many of us may sometimes get caught up in praying with ourselves in mind.

Consider the benevolence and kindness in these words:

May the sun always shine on your window-pane.

May a rainbow be certain to follow each rain.

May the hand of a friend always be near you.

May God fill your heart with gladness to cheer you.

Be mindful of the needs of others when you pray. Prayer brings immeasurable peace and good-will to both the one praying and to those prayed for.

Pray without ceasing. (1 Thessalonians 5:17)

Dear Jesus, help me remember others in my prayers, so that they may know Your peace.

Picture This!

Imagine yourself snapping photos while standing on a steel beam 40 or 50 stories above the ground. Outrageous?

For most of us, yes. But not for union iron-worker Gerard Suarez, known among his co-workers as "the Picture Guy."

Suarez uses photography to capture the progress of the sites he works on, as well as the detailed architecture he sees as the building rises.

"I love the lines, shadows, and light," explains Suarez. Often, he gives the photos to his co-workers as mementos of their work.

The most unlikely settings can hold the beauty of detail. Step out of the busy pace of your life to appreciate them. The beauty may surprise you.

Behold the beauty of the Lord. (Psalm 27:4)

Gracious Lord, remind me to take time to be thankful for the smallest of blessings.

When Fathers Go to Work

Do businesses support family life? 1500 chief executive officers and human relations directors were asked how much paternity leave is appropriate. Their response? 63 per cent said none!

A survey of fathers revealed that 30 percent had turned down promotion or transfers because it would have reduced the time they have to spend with families.

James Levine, author of *Working Fathers: New Strategies for Balancing Work and Family,* says, "I know of men who say they have a meeting across town when they're really going to pick up their kid from day care. These guys are trapped by an old-fashioned corporate culture, and they blame that culture. But they're a part of it. And unless they're willing to make clear that they have family needs, they perpetuate the cycle."

No one wants to risk a job. Yet if enough people let companies know that they need some flexibility to do a good day's work and raise a healthy family, we would all be better off.

Is not this the carpenter's son? Is not His mother called Mary? And are not His brothers...(and) all His sisters with us? (Matthew 13:55,56)

Father, help me to love and care for my family and to assist other families, too.

Boys and "Bang!"

Lisa Suhay watched as a first-grader pointed a stick at her 4-year-old son's forehead and yelled, "Bang! I just blew your head off, and you're dead now." Suhay and her friend, the mother of the other child, both flinched, as they had just been discussing what could be done to prevent teenage shooting sprees.

Ironically, Suhay had recently read an article that told parents, in essence, not to worry. Young boys practice "Bang, you're dead!" as a means of making contact with the world around them. It's natural, said the article, for them to shoot first and ask questions later. Suhay doesn't buy it. She's also convinced children can be steered past gunplay, but that it takes patience and constant, consistent directives on the part of parents.

Lisa Suhay wants her sons to be offended at the sight of a gun. "I want them to be afraid, indignant and alive," she says.

Guns and violence. The issues are not going away. It's time to make choices for ourselves and our children.

Agree with God and be at peace. (Job 22:21)

Continue to inspire us, Jesus, Prince of Peace.

An Inner City Pied Piper

On Chicago's South Side, the Robert Taylor Homes, two-dozen 16-story buildings form one of the largest public-housing complexes in the world and a monument to what ails parts of urban America.

A small, brick firehouse in this complex is home to Engine Company 16 and a haven for neighborhood children. The firemen have taken the local young people under their wing. "These children are our children," says Rocky Morris. "This is almost the only place...where they're safe."

Firefighter Kirkland Flowers took bicycles found on the street and started repairing them. As word spread about his linking the awarding of those bikes to school attendance—bicycles started pouring in from around the city. Attendance at the local school climbed.

Flowers takes community involvement seriously, saying, "If we don't do this, where are these kids going to go?"

We all have neighborhood responsibilities. How are you meeting yours?

Love does no wrong to a neighbor. (Romans 13:10)

Help us be a part of the larger community, Lord.

The Basics of Staying Fit

Let's face it, as we age we realize we can't push our bodies as hard as we used to. Fortunately, staying in good physical and mental shape isn't as difficult as we sometimes think it is.

Stay Active: s–t–r–e–t–c–h your muscles every morning. Take the stairs, walk the dog, go dancing. Accumulate 30 minutes of consistent, moderate exercise daily.

Control Stress: Try heart rate monitoring, yoga or meditation. Even taking a walk and concentrating on the moment helps.

Eat Right: Eat a low fat breakfast, five servings of fruits and vegetables daily; and drink at least 8 cups of water.

Lose Weight. Gradual mid-life weight gain is normal, but be "mindful" in your eating. Mix diet with exercise to lose and/or keep off weight. Treat God's great gift, your body, with respect.

You clothed me with skin and flesh, and knit me together with bones and sinews. You have granted me life and steadfast love, and Your care has preserved my spirit. (Job 10:11-12)

Enable me to reverence Your gift of my body, Creator.

Who Says New Yorkers Aren't Kind?

Justifiably or not, New York City has a reputation as a place where you cannot get service with a smile. Yet, every day some New Yorkers dispel this belief through their exemplary kindness.

Take florist Eun Jean Choi and her husband, who offer to accept packages for neighbors who are at work.

There's also Carlos Cortes, the owner of a bicycle shop. He is so devoted to his customers that he makes a daily ride through his local park to sweep up glass and clear branches and rocks from the cycling path so no cyclists will be injured.

Elevator operator Fernando Gomez spruces up his elevator with holiday decorations, lights and costumes for every season. "I do it for the kids [who ride the elevator]," he admits.

Stereotypes abound. Yet, each day countless individuals act to defy such preconceived notions.

Shatter a few preconceived notions yourself.

Do not judge by appearances, but judge with right judgment. (John 7:24)

Teach me how to accept the people I meet as unique individuals, Father Creator.

One Woman's Gift

Osceola McCarty died at the age of 91 in 1999.

Four years earlier, she had bequeathed her life savings of $150,000 to endow a scholarship for needy students at the University of Southern Mississippi. Not a remarkable sum in itself. But Osceola McCarty, of Hattiesburg, Mississippi, made her living doing other people's laundry.

Concerning her bequest she said, "I'm giving it away so that the children won't have to work so hard, like I did."

Miss McCarty became a celebrity after her selfless act and received an award from the United Nations, an honorary degree from Harvard, and an invitation to meet with the President of the United States. Another 600 donors, inspired by her charity, doubled the amount of her scholarship fund.

Miss McCarty said it all seemed pretty basic to her. "If you want to feel proud of yourself," she explained, "you've got to do things you can be proud of. Feelings follow actions."

A woman who fears the Lord is to be praised. (Proverbs 31:30)

Remind us, Lord, how generosity leads to generosity.

The Salt of the Earth

Common table salt, an important substance since ancient times, can be harmful if we use too much or if we don't get enough.

In vulnerable individuals, overdoing sodium intake is said to lead to high blood pressure, heart attacks and strokes as well as kidney disease. Many try to limit salt intake as part of a healthier diet.

But having no salt in the body is distinctly unhealthy. Sweat and tears are salty. So is amniotic fluid. Salt has many bodily functions. For example, it is involved in maintaining proper fluid balance, muscle contraction, and blood flow.

Humankind has harvested salt from the sea and mined it from the ground. It has worked its way into our everyday language. A highway in Italy, the Via Salaria or Salt Way, got its start in Roman times. Originally, soldiers lined the way guarding salt traders because salt was a precious commodity and its carriers were subject to attack. Soldiers were paid in salt, hence the term "salary." An inefficient worker was "not worth his salt."

Jesus called his disciples the salt of the earth.

Salt is good; but if salt has lost its saltiness, how can you season with it? (Mark 9:50)

Keep us mindful of our worth, Father.

The Laborer is Worth Her or His Hire

Ever wonder what might be the benefits of being a missionary? Think of the thrill of living your life out of what you believe, your faith.

There are other benefits, too:

- experiencing another people and their humanity;
- seeing the Gospel through new eyes, the eyes of those who do not have the same understanding as you do;
- sharing your convictions with whole-souled joy by letting others see God working in your own life.

How can you, today...at home...on the job...at your house of worship...running the day's errands...commuting... be a missionary?

Go into all the world and proclaim the good news to the whole creation. (Mark 16:15)

Holy Spirit, enflame me with Your Pentecostal fervor to live out my faith.

Saving Our Winged Friends

Scott Weidensaul participates in what he calls "the world's largest, longest running study of wild animals and one of the most effective cooperative research projects ever undertaken."

What Weidensaul and thousands of other licensed scientists and volunteers do is bird banding. They temporarily capture migrating hawks, eagles, falcons, painted buntings, shorebirds and others so they can affix tiny leg bands with distinctive colors or markings. Bands are constructed not to bother or restrict the birds.

In this way, scientists can track the movements of birds, their behaviors and survival strategies. The ultimate purpose is to help birds to survive and thrive in an environment now dominated by humans and machines.

Weidensaul's work with birds leaves him with feelings of awe and respect for these "travelers that stitch together this wide-world." He also prays that they will always grace the skies.

The birds...neither sow nor reap nor gather into barns, and yet your heavenly Father feeds them. Are you not of more value than they? (Matthew 6:26)

Grant us an appreciation for birds and all animals, Jesus.

Winning It All

If you think that life is an all-or-nothing proposition, think again. We really do get a second chance at success, everyday. We just have to take advantage of it.

Rabbi Harold Kushner, author of the bestseller *When Bad Things Happen to Good People*, believes that. He says: "Life is not a spelling bee, where no matter how many words you have gotten right, if you make one mistake you are disqualified.

"Life is more like a baseball season, where even the best team loses one-third of its games and even the worst team has its days of brilliance. Our goal is not to go all year without ever losing a game. Our goal is to win more than we lose, and if we can do that consistently enough, then when the end comes, we will have won it all."

Rejoice in your "days of brilliance." And never give up on your dreams or on yourself. God hasn't. Why should you?

Fear God, and keep His commandments. (Ecclesiastes 12:13)

Why is it so easy to quit on myself? Why won't I give myself the benefit of the doubt? Help me, Spirit of Counsel, to trust You and to trust myself to do Your will.

Making Texts Available to More

When the ancient Library at Alexandria, Egypt, which contained the greatest collection of books in antiquity, was burned, the loss was incalculable.

Determined to avoid a similar disaster, dedicated academics have been placing some of the earliest writings in English on microfilm. Eugene Power, a Michigan microfilm entrepreneur, has covered nearly 80 percent of all books printed in England between 1475 and 1700.

This early English collection is only a fraction of the company's 5.5 billion page microfilm archive, which includes newspapers, dissertations and other scholarly materials scheduled for on-line access in coming years. Many students can read the same work at the same time when needed. And, there is no chance of damage to ancient or rare texts.

It has been said that knowledge is power. It is certainly true that, used well, it is a stepping stone to wisdom.

(Jesus) went to the synagogue on the Sabbath day, as was His custom. He stood up to read, and the scroll of the prophet Isaiah was given to Him. (Luke 4:16-17)

Lord, thank You for the gift of writing and the ability to read and understand it.

Pages of a Life

Thomas Merton may be the most celebrated spiritual writer of the 20th century. Yet, many who have read his books do not realize how much he gave of himself to teach others.

After his accidental death in 1968, publishers began gathering the extraordinary works of this Trappist monk.

Today, nearly 6,000 pages of his writings have been published; 50 of his books are still in print.

His works include collections of poems, literary criticisms, five volumes of letters to 1,800 recipients, and nearly seven volumes of his journal. Even his lecture notes are being considered for publication!

Do you keep a journal of your life? ...your experiences? ...joys? ...sorrows? ...dreams? ...fears? ...hopes?

Keeping a daily journal will, over time, give you a better perspective on your life and help you see where you are going.

Those who live many years should rejoice in them all. (Ecclesiastes 11:8)

Holy Spirit, help me gain perspective on my life and where I'm going.

Volunteering: Giving and Getting

Students at Philadelphia's St. Joseph Prep volunteer two weeks each year to help poor communities and their residents.

During their service in the southwestern Appalachian community of Ivanhoe, Virginia, the students repaired public buildings and private homes, cleared overgrown vegetation, and painted seniors' homes.

They also planted trees and performed such home maintenance chores as applying sealant to mobile home roofs and delivering firewood.

One student, Chris Geschke, said, "They didn't have much materially to give, but they gave so much." Another student said he and his classmates experienced a world previously unknown to them.

Volunteering is more than just doing, it's receiving the generosity of others.

**Be rich in good works, generous.
(1 Timothy 6:18)**

Give me, dear God, the courage to put my convictions into action.

Laugh and the World Laughs with You

You don't normally picture a medical doctor in a clown nose and oversized shoes, but the old adage, "Laughter is the best medicine" is a prescription for health that works. Maybe it was a doctor who first said it.

Science has discovered that a hearty chuckle can actually give your immune system a boost, which helps in fighting disease. Laughter also decreases the levels of "stress hormones" in the body that may cause ulcers, high blood pressure and headaches. Levels of interferon-gamma increased significantly in patients after watching a funny video.

We develop the ability to laugh at 4 months, our sense of humor kicks in around age 3; kindergartners laugh up to 300 times a day and adults only 15! This God given anodyne seems to vanish as we grow older, and our body neglects its own built in cure.

Perhaps we should all remain children, and laugh our troubles away.

Whoever becomes humble like this child is the greatest in the kingdom of heaven.
(Matthew 18:4)

Lord, make me child-like without becoming childish.

When Brian Moved In

Brian Raymond and Zach Woodward had been best buddies since third grade. They stayed close even when it became clear that something was terribly wrong at Brian's house.

As Brian entered his sophomore year in high school, his mother, divorced from his father for some time, entered a local mental hospital. Brian had no place to go and turned to his friend Zach who turned to his parents. "Could Brian live here?" was Zach's question. The answer: "Yes."

Over the next two years, Brian became emancipated from his family. By senior year in high school, he was choosing among college engineering programs.

His time with the Woodwards was the most "home" he had ever known, Brian says. Each morning, although it is a most hectic time, Mrs. Woodward made pancakes–especially for Brian and Zach. "The boys will remember the pancakes for the rest of their lives," Mrs. Woodward says.

Surely they–Brian especially–will remember far more than that.

Be hospitable to one another. (1 Peter 4:9)

When You appear at the door, Lord, knocking to enter, help me recognize and admit You.

The Safest Sex

"There are more important things in life than just having a boyfriend on your arm," says one 18-year-old. She is one of twenty teen-members of, "La Familia." Group members promise to abstain from sexual activity before marriage.

Maria Cardona directs the group in a Bronx, New York, parish. "I've seen miracles here," she says. "This group teaches them to value themselves as individuals and realize that their bodies are sacred," Cardona explains.

And Moses Rodriguez, 17, notes that since being a part of La Familia, his skill at communicating with others has improved and his relationship with God is deeper.

The group is also its own support system. Eighteen-year old Jenine Cruz said that she never felt "such a closeness," adding, "the chastity promise does more than just get you to lead a chaste life. You get closer to God and the people around you."

You were bought with a price; therefore glorify God in your body. (1 Corinthians 6:20)

Thank You, Creator, for making me to know You, love You and serve You.

Color No Barrier to Respect

Growing up in the segregated South, "Pee Wee" Reese might have turned a cold shoulder when Jackie Robinson broke the color barrier and joined the Brooklyn Dodgers in 1947. He didn't.

Reese, a noted shortstop and team captain, refused to sign a petition by teammates who didn't want to play Major League baseball with a black man—no matter how much his talent would add to the team.

During one game in which fans were jeering Robinson, Reese made a gesture that spoke volumes. He walked over to his teammate and put his hand on his shoulder, thereby silencing the crowd.

Reese treated Robinson as a talented teammate. The two respected one another.

Humankind is still learning that we're all equal and precious in God's eyes.

Have we not all one father? Has not one God created us? (Malachi 2:10)

God, give us the courage to take a stand for justice.

Something Old, Something New

Where can hand-me-downs give a pick-me-up? At Mary Purdy's New York City apartment, that's where.

For nine years, the actress has been hosting an annual clothes-trading party right in her West Side apartment. Here, more than 30 women exchange items, then donate all unclaimed pieces to the Salvation Army.

"It's a social party...we get nice clothes, and donate to a worthy cause," says Purdy.

An old saying advises, "When life gives you lemons, make lemonade."

The ability to derive something positive and uplifting from all situations is a unique gift. Consider the good that can be discovered in each of life's events.

If a brother or sister is naked and lacks daily food...yet you do not supply their bodily needs, what is the good of that? (James 2:15,16)

Dear God, help me see You in everyone I meet.

Taking Care of Aging Parents

"My dad is gone. He's here, but he's not. I want to cry," noted *Time* magazine writer Cathy Booth in an article about adult children caring for parents who are declining physically and mentally.

Ms. Booth's father, once an architect, could no longer live alone. A few years before, the writer had taken on the role of caregiver for her mother who was dying from Lou Gehrig's disease.

"I'm hardly the only one going through this experience," writes Ms. Booth. "The number of Americans 85 and older has nearly tripled since 1960, to 4 million, and will more than double that over the next 30 years."

Families face challenges and even heart-wrenching decisions when elderly members are no longer able to take care of themselves.

Seek advice and support while going through this crisis. And, realize you're not alone.

Those who respect their father will have a long life; and those who honor their mother obey the Lord. (Sirach 3:6)

God, give us the strength to care for loved ones.

New Horizons

The members of New Horizons have been getting together once a week for eighteen years, enjoying each other's company, watching movies, dancing, and playing games. They celebrate holidays like St. Valentine's Day and Halloween, and each year, they take a road trip together.

New Horizons, a group of mentally and physically challenged adults, exists because Judge Rebecca Jackson is committed to them.

"I got the idea to start a weekly social program so adults with disabilities could meet and make friends." Volunteers from her church helped her launch the organization, but today, the judge, her husband, and their three sons see to it that the group continues to meet.

Judge Jackson says the friends she has come to love through New Horizons give her "the closest thing to God's unconditional love. They really care about me," she explains. "No matter how much I give to them, I always get much more in return."

The measure you give will be the measure you get back. (Luke 6:38)

Lord, keep us open to Your presence in every person.

Atop Old Jerusalem

Visitors to Jerusalem's Old City have an interesting and unique way to view this city so crammed with religious and secular history.

Tourists and others can walk on top of the massive stone walls of the Old City. These walls date from the Romans and even earlier. After entering from the Jaffa Gate, the Citadel or the Damascus Gate, one can look down on churches, mosques, synagogues, souqs (markets) and homes jammed on top of each other (sometimes literally).

You can see roofs, spires, domes and minarets; postage stamp–sized gardens; hushed courtyards and cloisters; step-streets and alleys; imagine ancient life; and see modern life going on below.

Viewing Jerusalem's Old City from atop its walls is a special way to see it. In fact, viewing anything from a different perspective can be a real eye-opener. Try it.

I was glad when they said to me, 'Let us go to the house of the Lord!' Our feet are standing within your gates, O Jerusalem. (Psalm 122:1-2)

God, encourage me to broaden my horizons.

Commitment to Loving Kindness

In order to encourage readers to believe in their own power to effect positive change, the editors of *Self* magazine challenged readers to keep a journal recording their acts of generosity for 100 days.

The magazine suggested those who choose to participate direct their selfless acts towards four categories: friends and family; difficult people in their lives (people from the first two categories might overlap); the general public; and themselves. The editors said it was important to focus on all four categories.

"Otherwise, you might spend several hours a week serving soup in a homeless shelter but snap mindlessly at your mother," they wrote.

The magazine encouraged readers to begin by showering loving kindness, based on a Buddhist meditation, on themselves: "This may seem self-indulgent, but the practice is based on the belief that we can't share our bounty or care for others when we feel uncared for ourselves."

You shall love your neighbor as yourself. (Matthew 19:19)

Almighty God, give us eyes to see our own hearts with Your love.

Praising through Music

Denis Grady believes God is leading him from a life of addiction to one of songwriting and music. "God loves singing," says Grady. "He wants you to praise Him singing."

Grady, 47, won praise for his first album, "Running Too Long." It's somewhat autobiographical and includes lines which came to him while he was in a rehabilitation center.

"When the Lord dealt with my addiction, the hell ended," said Grady.

While Grady's music is categorized as Gospel, it might also be found in the Country section. "In the traditional country, there's a lot of room to sing about God."

Denis Grady sees singing as a path God steered him towards. "I enjoy it. I say let's have fun with it. God does not have a shortage of joy."

Praise Him with trumpet...lute and harp!... tambourine...strings and pipe! (Psalm 150:3-4)

Lord, let me sing Your praises.

'Tis a Gift to Be Simple

This wise Shaker hymn, know to many through Aaron Copeland's "Appalachian Spring," reminds us to be open to simplicity.

- Be up to see the sky lighten, birds twitter and chirp for the first time that day.
- Visit small, unusual museums.
- Use mass transit.
- Get to the ballpark. Have a hot dog and conversation with friends before the game.
- Visit a green market or wholesale florist just for the beauty.
- Go for long evening walks with your spouse or friends or yourself. Notice the sky, the light, as day fades into night.
- Try beachcombing. Or go to the beach in late afternoon. The sun will not be as hot; the crowds lighter.

Simplicity makes us aware of our place in God's world .

From the greatness and beauty of created things comes a corresponding perception of their Creator. (Wisdom of Solomon 13:5)

Thank You, God, for creation's beauties and life's joys.

Bread and Wine on the Moon

Did you know that the first liquid poured and the first bread eaten on the moon were the Communion elements?

In 1969, when Neil Armstrong and Buzz Aldrin descended to the lunar surface in the Apollo 11 spacecraft Eagle, Aldrin was carrying two special containers. One, left on the moon's surface, contained the text of Psalm 8. It had been given by Pope Paul VI to the United States as a symbol of God's role in space exploration.

The other container held a small bit of bread and tiny chalice of wine that Aldrin had brought from a special Communion service held the week before at his Presbyterian church. He had wondered whether it might be possible to take Communion on the moon. His pastor enthusiastically supported the idea and arrangements were made.

Aldrin read the words illustrating his trust that in exploring space, humankind was acting in God's name. "He who abides in me, and I in him, bears much fruit, for without Me, you can do nothing." Then Aldrin consumed the Bread and Wine.

Abide in Me as I abide in you. (John 15:4)

God, abide with me wherever I am.

Christianity Redefined

English author G. K. Chesterton (1874–1936) had a unique definition of Christianity, a romance.

Chesterton believed God wants us to feel wondrously happy in the world, much in the way one does when falling in love. And, like many Catholic theologians who followed him, Chesterton also believed that spiritual reliance on God was, above all, "fun."

It's not that Chesterton refuted logic and reason. But he did argue the need to acknowledge the limits of reason. Not surprisingly, Chesterton believed poetry was superior to logic.

What a beautiful way to define faith, a romance! One writer's view could help cast a new perspective on how you view your own relationship with God.

I found Him whom my soul loves. I held Him and would not let Him go. (Song of Songs 3:4)

Jesus, I pray that I may experience the joy and happiness of really knowing You.

On Arms, War and Violence

Just what is the human cost of war?

In the first half of the twentieth century, 50 percent of casualties were civilian. In the final ten years of the century, it was more than 90 percent. During the last decade two million children died in wars. Between four and five million were physically disabled. More than twelve million were made homeless and five million were made refugees.

Half of the world's nations spend more on the military than on health care.

These statistics come from the international peace organization Pax Christi.

Each man, woman and young person has an obligation to work in some way for peace – in home and heart, in community and world. We have no right to give lip service, saying "Blessed are the peacemakers," while doing nothing to deter violence.

Pray today. Act today. Be a person of peace.

Wisdom from above is...peaceable, gentle, willing to yield...a harvest of righteousness is sown in peace for those who make peace. (James 3:17, 18)

Lead me to dedicate myself to peace, Jesus.

Talking to God

Teaching your children to pray can seem a daunting challenge. Too often we fall back on memorized prayers. But these can lack immediacy. Utilize the **ACTS**–Adoration, Confession, Thanksgiving and Supplication–formula:

Adoration: Begin with the phrase, "I love you God because you are…" The goal: elicit from children an attribute of God.

Confession: Offer a cue such as, "Lord, please forgive me for…" Encourage children to be specific. Participate so children learn that parents are sinners forgiven by God, just as they are.

Thanksgiving: Begin simply by thanking God for the good things that have happened during the day; special people in your lives; for having a good day.

Supplication: A big word for kids to grasp, but they do. Divide it into praying for others and praying for yourself.

Do not grow weary when you pray. (Sirach 7:10)

May children know the power of prayer, Master.

"A Brighter Tomorrow"

Antoinette "Toni" Jones is one amazing 13-year-old. After surviving nearly three years in a refugee camp in Sierra Leone, Toni, now a student in Catholic school in Jamaica, began a program to help other refugee children.

Naming her project "A Brighter Tomorrow," Toni started writing letters to the Pope, to the United Nations High Commission Office for Refugees (UNHC), and to Bloomingdale's Department Store. Bloomingdale's donated children's books and other items, which the UNHC distributes in plastic bags to boys and girls ages 4 to 15.

Because she and her family saw preteen boys being drafted into the Liberian Civil War, Toni wants countries to agree not to turn children into soldiers. "I want them to have an awareness for those who are less fortunate."

Jones remembers "what it is like to not have what I need." There's a lot to be learned from this youngster's example of empathy, sympathy and grass roots activism.

See what almsgiving accomplishes. (Tobit 14:11)

Inspire me to provide for those in need, generous Lord.

Using Obstacles as Stepping Stones

Achieving top scorer status for the first two seasons of the Women's National Basketball Association (WNBA) was something few people believed would ever happen for Cynthia "Coop" Cooper.

When she began playing, she didn't have a jumpshot. She couldn't use her left hand to shoot or dribble and rarely scored a three-pointer—all essential for a high scorer.

In spite of all of this, Cooper didn't give up. She viewed her weaknesses as fuel to practice incessantly. Eventually, she led the Houston Comets to two successive championships, and was named league MVP for both years.

Today, her perseverance has led her to what promises to be an equally successful second career as a corporate spokesperson.

Tenacity isn't something we're all born with. Sometimes we actively choose to develop our perseverance as we grow.

Bear fruit with patient endurance. (Luke 8:15)

Father, remind me that sometimes, the best way to use the talents You gave me is through hard work.

"Real" Age

Are you a person who "wears their years well?"

Some people manage to slow the aging process. Often a septuagenarian who looks and feels ten years younger will attribute it to good genes. That's part, but not all, of the story.

The choices we make about eating, exercise and lifestyle are more important. Those who remain active, alert and healthy are usually moderate in drinking and eating.

According to Johns Hopkins University cardiologist Dr. David Myerson, "to remain young and active when you're older...don't smoke."

Finally, maintain a support system of family and friends, and put laughter in your life.

Life is for living. Get on with it. Seize *each* day!

In everything you do be moderate. (Sirach 31:22)

Help me remain young in heart and mind, Great Giver.

More Suggestions for Handling Stress

This is the intermediate course in stress management.

- Keep a duplicate car key in your wallet; bury one in the yard (remember where it's buried!). Give one to a friend or neighbor.
- Give a duplicate house key to a friend, neighbor, or relative who can be trusted to respect your privacy.
- Practice preventive maintenance on your relationships, your body, your teeth and eyes, your car.
- Exercise for a least half-an-hour a day.
- Eat well–that means at home–85% of the time and eat lightly.
- Be kind to the unlovely, the irritable, the unkind.
- Don't make too many promises. When you do, keep them.
- Turn off the TV, phone, pager, computer, fax, cell phone, and enjoy the quiet.

Put these into practice and enjoy life more.

The Lord...will sustain you. (Psalm 55:22)

Calm me down, gracious Lord.

The Courage to Live

Dawn Anna could have died while giving birth to her youngest child or during brain surgery that forced her to learn to walk again. But she did not.

Ms. Anna had been the girls' volleyball coach for seven seasons at Columbine High School in Colorado. Then, on April 20, 1999, Dawn learned that her youngest child, Lauren, had been among those murdered by two fellow students.

She's coping, dedicating herself to making other people's kids safe in schools. "There are too many guns out there, way too many," she says. She's also planning a college scholarship for a Columbine student.

Meanwhile, Dawn Anna is having more health problems. But after her own two brushes with death she believes, "God was preparing me for Lauren's death."

God offers us comfort in our greatest pain. He offers Himself.

The Lord God will wipe away the tears from all faces. (Isaiah 25:7)

I have faith, Lord, increase it.

A Pressing Choice

As the millennium approached, the A&E Television Network launched an ambitious project: choosing the 100 most influential people of the past one thousand years.

The network's editorial board made the selections after polling nearly 400 journalists and taking into consideration the thoughts and comments of viewers who accessed their web site.

They named their top 100 in reverse order, leading up to the one person they felt had done the most to shape the world today. Among those chosen were Nicolaus Copernicus and Marie Curie, Joan of Arc and Walt Disney.

Near the end of the program, anchor Harry Smith finally announced the network's number one choice: Johann Gutenberg, developer of the printing press and movable type. He was a dedicated craftsman whose invention dramatically changed the world.

We may never be famous, but we do have the opportunity to change the world for the better.

Heaven is like the master...who brings out... what is new and what is old. (Matthew 13:52)

Keep us focused on our calling, Lord, no matter how humble it may seem.

Too Close for Comfort

Is there such a thing as too much intimacy?

Can "too close" mean an end to "comfort"?

Discretion is a much-needed commodity these days. That means being discreet about our own life and about the lives of others as well.

Consider, for example, the harm you do to others by gossiping, and consider too the harm you do to yourself. A reputation for being able to keep your mouth shut is attractive. The opposite is not.

Even in our most intimate relationships there's always a need to think about what you're going to say, how it will sound and how it might affect your listener.

It never hurts to ask yourself why you want to tell your partner something that you had not previously revealed. The impulse to "share" is sometimes the wish to unload or, even worse, the concealed wish to hurt. Thinking it over—whether it is about a fact of your life or another's—is never a mistake.

A gossip reveals secrets. (Proverbs 20:19)

Teach me, Jesus, to act as You would, to treat others as You did.

From One Person to the World

In the late 1930s, ecology and conservation were hardly household words. Except in Aldo Leopold's home, that is.

It was Leopold who would spend his mornings writing in a little notebook, recording the birds he sighted, the migration of geese, and the blooming of flowers and foliage. He was the first person to argue for a "land ethic," and the collective responsibility among all citizens to care for animals and the land.

A forester, wildlife expert, professor and visionary, Leopold described himself as an ecologist, in a time when the nation had barely heard the word.

Leopold pioneered a movement and articulated a new way to look at and care for God's creatures; a poignant reminder of what one individual can accomplish in a lifetime.

The Lord...formed the earth and made it (He established it; ...He formed it to be inhabited!). (Isaiah 45:18)

Teach me respect for all that You've created, Sovereign Lord.

Wizard of Advertising

The advertising firm of Ogilvy and Mather has offices worldwide. But when David Ogilvy started the agency, his odds of success seemed to be anything but favorable.

He had flunked out of Oxford University, tried his hand at farming and selling door-to-door, and worked in a hotel kitchen.

But in time he would introduce the world to Commander Whitehead in ads for Schweppes beverages and to the man with the eye-patch who wore Hathaway shirts. He became not only a leader in his field, but a legend.

And whenever David Ogilvy put someone in charge of a new office he gave this advice: "If each of us hires people who are smaller than we are, we shall become a company of dwarfs. But if each of us hires people who are bigger than we are, we shall become a company of giants."

Are you afraid of having a person who is better than you are at something "show you up?" Learn from the best and the brightest. You may grow into a giant.

Ezra had his heart set to study the Law of the Lord. (Ezra 7:10)

Dear God, there are times when I feel small and insignificant. Nurture me.

Veggie Tales

Do you know Larry the Cucumber and Bob the Tomato of *Veggie Tales*? It's one of the fastest selling children's videos thanks to the creators' desire to produce entertaining tapes with religious meaning.

Mike Nawrocki was en route to becoming a pediatrician; instead he plays a cucumber. He and his close friend and fellow puppeteer from St. Paul Bible College, Paul Vischer, pursued the idea of serving people by creating kids' videos. Could they make it work? All indications are, yes!

Vischer insists that the videos were not created as a substitute for formal religious education, but rather as an alternative to Saturday morning cartoons.

Veggie Tales grew out of a desire of two men to serve and to teach. As Mike Nawrocki says, "From the outset, what we wanted was to make a difference…to change kids' lives."

How are you making a difference?

You are the light of the world. (Matthew 5:14)

May I use my creativity to bring light to the world, Holy Spirit.

Relieving Chernobyl

On April 26, 1986, 190 tons of highly reactive uranium was released into the atmosphere over Chernobyl, the Ukraine, a region of the former Soviet Union. The youngest victims of that tragedy have not been forgotten.

More than 450 children from the most contaminated parts of the region have had some reprieve from the ongoing effects of the radiation through the Chernobyl Children USA, Inc. Project. Run by Rev. Robert Bowers, the interfaith effort gives young people the opportunity to receive free medical treatment, find fun and clean air and experience family life in the United States.

Doctors have found that for every month a child is away from the radiation, two years are added to his or her life. "We want them to know they will always be in our prayers," Rev. Bowers says. "That is why this project started and why it will continue."

Faith is expressed through prayer and works.

[Jesus] took her by the hand and said to her, 'Talitha cum'. (Mark 5:41)

Father, forgive us for poisoning ourselves, our children and the future.

An Actor Who Cares

A simple house call to an ailing actor "was the luckiest thing to happen to about 20,000 kids," says Mayer Heiman.

Dennis Quaid was in New Orleans, starring in, *The Big Easy*, when the flu bug bit. Impressed and grateful that Dr. Heiman made house calls, he told the internist to stay in touch. A few weeks later, Heiman phoned Quaid and asked if he wanted to check out The International Hospital for Children (IHC). The doctor had founded the non-profit organization in Honduras to bring medical care to areas of the world without it.

Quaid obliged and observed IHC in action: "You see the kids and the need and how simple it would be to help them."

As an IHC advisory board member, Quaid is involved at every step. He says the hands-on nature of his contribution makes it the perfect way for him to give something back.

One individual can't solve the world's problems. But one day and one effort at a time can make a dent.

Love one another as I have loved you. (John 15:12)

Help me to help make a difference, Great Healer.

A Walk on the Wild Side

Can wildflowers tame people? It's hard to say what impact plants, flowers and gardening have on a person. Yet it all seems to be good for Adrian Foulkes and fellow inmates at Her Majesty's Prison Leyhill in England.

Foulkes, nearing parole on a sentence for murder, is one of seven prisoners who won a gold medal in the Hampton Court Palace Flower Show. Their entry in this year's extravaganza staged by the Royal Horticultural Society was entitled "Take a Walk on the Wild Side."

The prisoners help plant the flowers, vegetables and trees in the display, which will be viewed by horticulturalists and garden designers.

While they repay a debt to society, the inmates "provide much pleasure to the gardening public," says the director of the annual shows. They make "a valuable contribution to horticulture."

O Lord, how manifold are Your works! In wisdom You have made them all; the earth is full of Your creatures. (Psalm 104:24)

Help us to appreciate nature, Father.

Amateur Makes a Major Impact

John Snyder showed once again that amateurs with a love of their subject can make contributions that leave professionals in awe.

A chemical engineer whose hobby was cartography, Snyder solved what has been referred to as one of the most difficult map-making problems of the 20th Century.

It seems that once NASA started launching satellites which circled the earth collecting vast amounts of data about the terrain below, there was a need to translate all that new information into the language of standard maps.

It was a tricky problem. Snyder, who died in 1998, credited others with the original idea at the basis of the solution. But there seems little doubt that his so-called amateur tinkering made it all workable.

The love and intelligence we put into a project can make all the difference in the world.

Let us work for the good of all. (Galatians 6:10)

Help us, Lord, to share our passions with others.

Childhood stress, then and now

If you believe that youngsters have felt stress only recently, here's a surprising quote.

"The prevailing tendency of modern civilized life is the over stimulation of children. This tendency pervades our whole educational system. It permeates juvenile literature, is manifest in childhood recreations, and has invaded the home.

"Such overstraining and stimulation cannot fail to cause harmful effects during childhood and produce nervous temperament later in life. In our environment of modern-civilized life, the ear and the brain are being shocked by the screams of the locomotive, the noise of the streetcar, the rumblings of the heavy wagons on stony pavement."

— Journal of the American Medical Society,
December 10, 1898.

Is this world tougher on young people than in 1898? In many ways, yes. But parents and children can still experience a rich home life if they make the effort to have a close, strong family.

House and wealth are inherited from parents. (Proverbs 19:14)

Child of Bethlehem, guide the children and parents of this generation and the next.

What's Your Mission?

Richard N. Bolles' popular book, *What Color Is Your Parachute?*, has become a classic among job-seekers.

He is also the author of *How to Find Your Mission in Life*. In it he writes:

"There are all different kinds of voices calling you to all different kinds of work. The challenge is to determine which is the voice of God–and which is the voice of society, the superego, or self-interest. By and large, a good rule for finding your life's mission is this: The kind of work God usually calls you to do is the kind of work that: (a) you need most to do and, (b) the world needs most to have done.

"Where is your mission? The place God calls you is the place where your deep gladness meets the world's deep hunger."

These are not easy concepts to confront. But doing so may be the first step in fulfilling the mission God has for you.

Speak, for Your servant is listening.
(1 Samuel 2:31)

I need a life with meaning. Guide me, God.

To Everything There Is a Season

"There are times when, mysteriously, nothing goes right," observed *Good Housekeeping* columnist Peggy Noonan. But there are also "times when, for no reason, nothing goes wrong."

All of us have experienced those wonderful moments when everything with our family and friends and work is going well.

By the same token, the phrase "when it rains, it pours," comes out of the universal experience of one disappointment after another. No matter how hard we try to think positively, at times we seem unable to find success and happiness.

When Noonan enjoyed what she called "a good season," she was not concerned that it would eventually come to an end.

"The most important things happen to you in the sowing times," she said, "because that's where you learn the things you need–strength, faith, patience, endurance, optimism."

Noonan suggests that in a good season, "It's good to share the bounty."

Those who are generous are blessed. (Proverbs 22:9)

Give us the wisdom, Holy Spirit, to embrace all the seasons of our life.

Pulp Action

As a chemical engineer, Al Wong is more than aware of the industrial air and water pollution, devastation of trees and forests, and overall waste caused by traditional paper production.

In 1983 he founded Arbokem, Inc., a Vancouver-based research company seeking an alternative source of fiber for pulp.

A decade later, the firm had devised a way to turn straw discarded by local farmers into papers and newsprint that wouldn't pollute the way traditional paper production does.

How did it happen? While traveling on business, Wong happened to see harvested fields dotted with bales of straw. He saw not the useless leftovers of the harvest, but potential raw material for paper. He laughed, "How come nobody in the country sees this as a resource?"

One person's waste is the opportunity of a lifetime to another. Look around you—you could find potential for success in the most unlikely places.

Commit your work to the Lord. (Proverbs 16:3)

Holy Spirit, inspire my imagination to transform problems into opportunities.

Heart to Heart

Researchers have now proven that volunteering on a regular basis improves self-esteem, increases well-being, and lowers stress.

Author Liz Rhoades cites John Cardozo as a living example. After a heart attack at age 45, Cardozo realized he would have to diet, quit smoking, and begin to exercise.

When angina returned despite his efforts, Cardozo turned to Dr. Dean Ornish who not only prescribes diet and light exercise, but also emphasizes the need for his patients to rely on and reinforce love in their lives.

Says Ornish: "when you help other people, you also help free yourself from loneliness and pain and isolation."

Cardozo volunteered to teach adults to read and offered his services to senior citizens in need of tax advice. Has it helped?

"I'm in better health than I've ever been," says the 75-year-old racquetball player.

God...breathed into Adam's nostrils the breath of life. (Genesis 2:7)

Thank You, Creator, for the way Your love in us brings a multitude of blessings.

"Niche" Samaritans

The volunteers at the Inn of the Good Samaritan, in the Dominican Republic, uncovered a unique and not-so-obvious need.

Often, it is simply confusion in navigating the health care system that prevents the sick from getting the help they desperately need. The Inn offers the sick guidance in accessing medical care and supplies.

The missionaries assist those who are illiterate, those who are too frightened to go into the capital city for treatment, or those who simply need advice and direction in following doctors' orders, taking medicine, etc.

These missionaries have found their "niche" and have helped save lives. Consider the endless possibilities the world holds for helping those in need. What single, small thing can you do today to answer the call of someone with a unique need?

Help the poor for the commandment's sake. (Sirach 29:9)

God, give me the ability to see hidden opportunities to serve the needy.

Gym-less Fitness

Spreading? No time, less money, and even less energy or enthusiasm or whatever it takes to get into gym gear and actually go to a gym?

All's not lost. According to Health and Human Services Secretary Donna Shalala, "You don't have to train like an Olympic athlete to enjoy the benefits of a healthy lifestyle."

But you do need to use your body, not labor-saving gadgets. So...

- Turn off that dishwasher.
- Take the stairs at the office.
- Park the car a little farther from your destination each time and walk that distance.
- Take an after dinner amble.
- Do your own housework, even the bathroom and the windows.
- Bend, squat, stretch, reach as you grocery shop or look for books at the library or book store.
- Use a bike.

Get moving. Feel well. And, have f-u-n!

**Give yourself the esteem you deserve.
(Sirach 10:28)**

Creator, give me the courage to be less slothful.

The Courage of His Convictions

College freshman Wang Dan could have opted to focus on his studies and personal goals, and most of all, having fun. Instead, he summoned his courage to be at the forefront of the pro-democracy movement in his native China. That year, 1989, was marked by the Tiananmen Square massacre.

The image of Wang shouting support to his fellow students into a bullhorn the day of the massacre symbolizes his commitment to his beliefs. "Our interest in democracy was based on concerns like freedom of speech," explains Wang, now 30.

Although he was fortunate enough to have escaped the violence of the day, the young activist served nearly four years in prison and was jailed again soon after release for signing a human rights petition.

Acting on one's convictions demands strength, character, and courage. Your life and the lives around you are enriched and inspired whenever you put your beliefs into action.

Deal courageously. (2 Chronicles 19:11)

Lord God, give me a share of Your courage.

A Portrait of Life

Artist George Pocheptsov emigrated to the United States from the Ukraine when he was very young. His paintings now bring in $11,000 apiece. Most of his work depicts scenes of animals, people, and fanciful creatures.

Pocheptsov, better known as Georgie, is just seven years old.

With the help of a gallery owner who understands that the artist is still a child, Georgie draws for a few hours each day. As soon as it becomes a chore, however, his mother, Dubrava, sends him outside to play.

Dubrava's perspective? "He's good at drawing," she concedes, "but other children in his class can read better."

Dubrava never talks about the future with her son. She maintains that art does not have to be his whole life. As she told writer Beth Brophy, however, he will always be an artist. "Drawing is his passion," she explained. "It's in his soul."

There are varieties of gifts. (1 Corinthians 12:4)

Creator God, open our hearts to the people who will free us to use Your gifts to the fullest.

Forever Choices

Dr. Anthony Morgan, chairman and director of surgery at St. Francis Hospital in Hartford, Connecticut, has spent more than a dozen years as a trauma surgeon, much of it in pediatrics. He says he feels the pain of his patients more and more as he grows older.

"It hurts more because of the needless causes of pain that I see children do to themselves," he explains.

Morgan is referring to everything from children who ride bicycles without helmets to those who are under the influence of alcohol and drugs. He finds himself asking, "Where are the parents?"

Again and again, Morgan hears parents tell him they simply don't have the time to be involved in every aspect of their children's lives. But he doesn't accept that response.

"You must have the time for the rest of your life," he insists. "You are always a parent, whether your child is 4 months old, 4 years old, or 40."

Does your life reflect responsibility for the choices you have made?

Choose what is right. (Job 34:4)

Creator God, give us renewed enthusiasm.

The Stranger Who Was Really a Friend

On the 10th anniversary of her mother's death, visiting strangers was the last thing Myrtle Potter wanted to do.

So when her pastor asked her to be part of a team checking on people who hadn't been at church for a while, Potter politely replied, "Not today. I'm sorry."

Later Potter thought better of it. "For years after Mama died, I had met with her friends to laugh and talk, remembering her cheerful ways, her parties and how she made time to visit the housebound," she explained. "The word visit stung my conscience. I went back to the minister and told him I would help."

She was asked to visit 100-year-old Cora Heinecke. When Heinecke saw Potter, she said: "Lillian Layton's daughter? What a blessing!"

"Cora had been a close friend of my mother's! For more than an hour we talked about Mama," Potter says.

A good deed. A day to remember and make memories, too.

Do not hesitate to visit the sick. (Sirach 7:35)

Keep me open, Teacher, to others. For in them, I discover You.

The Aspirin Label Warning

When Dr. Douglas Reye died in 1977, few realized his importance.

While practicing at the Royal Alexandria Hospital in Sydney, Australia, Dr. Reye studied tissue from the body of a ten-month-old boy. He saw liver and brain damage he'd never seen before.

Over the next 11 years, Dr. Reye identified 20 more cases of what his colleagues nicknamed "Reye's syndrome."

Two decades later American epidemiologists linked Reye's syndrome to the use of aspirin to control fevers in children with viral infections. Word spread. The use of aspirin among children declined as did the incidence of Reye's syndrome. Warning labels are now the standard on all bottles of aspirin.

Dr. Reye's reports led to one of this century's major public health triumphs. And the doctor whose obituary in the Medical Journal of Australia was less than two lines now has his name on every aspirin bottle.

You never know how your contribution to this world will turn out. Contribute today.

Overcome evil with good. (Romans 12:21)

Help me to help good, Lord.

A Welcome "Welcome" for New Moms

For the hundreds of babies born each year in Franklin County, Ohio to parents without any health insurance, a new "Welcome Home" program can be a lifeline of support.

The county's Mount Carmel Outreach provides up to three free home visits by a registered nurse to qualifying new moms who lack sufficient health insurance. The visits include examining the newborn as well as the mom to see how both are progressing. A gift basket full of baby items and health information makes the visit especially welcome.

When you reach out to new mothers and fathers in your community, you're helping them do the hardest and most important job on earth, raising another human being.

As a mother comforts her child, so I will comfort you. (Isaiah 66:13)

May I have compassion for new moms and dads and the stresses they face, Lord of Life.

Everyday Life, Heroic Acts

Who is your hero or heroine? For television anchor Jack Ford, it is his mother.

"When you look to people who helped mold you, and got you to where you wanted to be, that's perhaps the best definition of a hero. My mother is mine," states Ford.

That's no surprise. His mother rescued him and his three siblings from a violent, abusive father, at a time (the 1950s) in which it was rare for a woman to raise children alone.

The family endured bankruptcy, homelessness and prolonged struggle, but Ford's mother never faltered. She took on three or four jobs at a time, and at 40 returned to college for her teaching degree. Ford attended Yale University and became an athlete and television anchor.

What is your definition of a hero? Someone courageous? Intelligent? Creative? Think of those who have helped you thus far in life. If possible, thank them. Importantly, imitate them. Mentor someone yourself.

I have set you an example, that you also should do as I have done. (John 13:15)

I pray that I may serve as an example to even just one person today, Lord.

The Healing Power of Animals

Increasing attention is being paid to the therapeutic use of animals in hospitals.

Patients respond to the unconditional love that these animals give. Whether it is a dwarf Hotot rabbit named Rosie, or a miniature horse, Petie, their visits to schools, hospitals and nursing homes raise patients' level of joy.

Ciara Jacobson was born with serious heart problems. Her mother scheduled her therapy to coincide with the visits of Petie. Now, it is not difficult at all to get the youngster enthused about her visits.

Francie Jonsson's 5'2" llama, Lizzy, sparked an unexpected reaction from an advanced Alzheimer's patient. He spent a long time running his fingers through her fur.

And Fluffanilla, a mule, rekindles empathy and caring among some abused teenagers.

Healing comes from all of God's creation—if we're open to it.

You save humans and animals alike, O Lord. (Psalm 36:6)

Lord, help me appreciate all creatures great and small.

Kids Lead Clean-Up Efforts

With their energy and idealism, teenagers have a lot to offer their communities. The key is to find a cause that engages their interest.

The Hunts Point Rangers, in red shirts and white helmets, patrol on bicycles in their Bronx neighborhood looking for environmental violations.

Trained by the State Department of Environmental Conservation, the teens look out for illegally dumped garbage, trucks with idling engines or other pollution problems.

"We caught a lot of trucks idling in the neighborhood, and though at first some of them would get upset, after awhile they would just take off," said Luis Quinones, 17. Adds Mike Perez, 15, "We feel good about what we're doing."

A DEC spokesperson acknowledged that the youngsters serve as "our eyes and ears." They provide an important service in an area with too few enforcement officers.

The Lord...formed the earth. (Isaiah 45:18)

Lord, inspire young people to improve their neighborhood.

Working for Change—on Both Sides

At 51, Dr. Theodore Ning, a prominent Denver urologist, and his wife, Connie, a psychotherapist, became full-time volunteers in Friendship Bridge. They founded the organization to assist the people of Vietnam where Dr. Ning had served as an Army doctor.

In 1988, as part of a personal mission, he went back there, accompanied by his wife. Together they looked at health conditions, particularly for Vietnamese mothers and their children. Twelve trips later, they had built Friendship Bridge, sending to the country 140 tons of medical supplies, establishing medical teaching centers and recruiting some 300 volunteers to staff those centers.

In addition, they managed to bring 30 Vietnamese medical professionals to Colorado for short-term study. "When people first get involved, they believe they're helping others," Dr. Ning explains. "Then they experience a deep personal transformation. This helps change people on both sides."

Clothe yourselves with compassion.
(Colossians 3:12)

Use me this day, Lord, to bring Your love and compassion to others.

Learning New Tricks

Books have been Jessie Sherer Abbott's passion since she first learned to read. "You can teach an old dog new tricks–from books," she claims. Among the hundreds of volumes she's collected:

The Bible. "It has it all," says Abbott: poetry, prose, romance and courage.

The Dictionary. Since college wasn't possible, "I became my own teacher, using the dictionary and every book I could get hold of."

The Little Engine That Could, for its message of "I think I can" that became her motto.

Bartlett's Familiar Quotations, "insight and inspiration from so many sources and great minds."

Gone With the Wind. The story of Scarlett O'Hara, "who though spoiled, was also a strong survivor."

Take a cue from one book lover, exercise your eyes, brain and imagination often.

**He read...the book of the Covenant.
(2 Chronicles 34:30)**

May the Bible and other books teach us, God.

"What Do You Need?"

A troubled Jodi Sellers called up WomanSafe Center in Faribault, Minnesota, for help getting out of a dangerous relationship. The woman who answered asked, "What do you need?"

With the help and encouragement of the Center's staff and volunteer advocates, Sellers found her way to safety.

Now she volunteers 25 hours a week at WomanSafe answering the hotline or accompanying battered women to court. She asks each woman, "What do you need?" For most, it has probably been a long time since anyone asked.

Sellers also believes in the power of prayer. She's amazed that even in their darkest hour many women express a strong faith in God. If they don't pray, Sellers prays for them.

Jodi Sellers reclaimed her life because people listened to her, and prayers were answered. Never underestimate the effects of listening—and the power of the ultimate Listener.

"Be opened." And immediately his ears were opened, his tongue was released. (Mark 7:34-35)

Spirit, open my heart to those in peril.

Wise Words

"Whoever does not see God in every place does not see God in any place," proclaims Rabbi Menachem Mendel of Kotzk.

His words are but one jewel in a recently-translated treasure trove of a thousand sayings by Hasidic teachers. Their collective insights can be found in *Hasidic Wisdom: Sayings from the Jewish Sages,* written by Simcha Raz and translated by Don Peretz Elkins and Jonathan Elkins.

Reviewer Frederic Brussat says the volume offers both common sense and glints of brilliance. He points to Rabbi Meir of Apta who writes, "Those who have no compassion for themselves have none for others either."

Inspired by the writings, Brussat encourages readers to enjoy the book, convinced the best attitude is one of gratitude. He notes the example of Rabbi Nachman of Bratslav who says: "One must dance each day and every day–whether in thought or action."

**Offer to God a sacrifice of thanksgiving.
(Psalm 50:14)**

Lord, let us hear You in our brothers and sisters.

Castles in the Air

Gail Borden was a creative tinkerer.

When he lost his young wife and 4-year old son to yellow fever in 1844, he spent years trying to invent a cure.

Later, he used a dehydration technique to preserve meat in biscuit form. His product was a miserable failure, leading to bankruptcy in 1852.

He built a terraqueous machine featuring sails that was to be at home on both land and sea. His efforts were laughable.

Undeterred, he told a friend that there was no use in looking back. "If I did," he quipped, "I should soon be dead or in a mad house."

Finally, Borden developed a vacuum technique to condense fresh milk prior to preserving it. In 1858, the Committee of the Academy of Medicine declared the product "unequaled" in purity, durability, and economy.

Today, Borden's Eagle Brand Condensed Milk and its trademark Elsie the Cow are part of the Borden Family of Companies doing $3 billion in business each year.

Happy are those who persevere. (Daniel 12:12)

Savior, guide me.

Knowing How to Give

The pro football wide receiver Jerry Rice of the San Francisco 49ers is known as one of the sport's hardest workers. Over the last few years, he's given similar effort to helping sick and underprivileged children in his community.

Just after giving birth to their third child, his wife Jackie began hemorrhaging. She was in critical condition for a time, but survived. That inspired Rice to work more closely with the March of Dimes.

Rice has appeared every year since at the San Francisco March of Dimes Walkathon, and is currently honorary chair of the March of Dimes WalkAmerica. He and his wife volunteer their time on the weekends and give generous amounts of money.

This gifted athlete has learned that, as he puts it, "There's more to life than football. Those doctors bent over backwards to help us. That's what I'm trying to do with the March of Dimes."

What person or organization needs the gift of your time, talents and, if possible, treasure?

A generous person has cause to rejoice. (Sirach 40:14)

Show us how to be generous, Holy Spirit.

Making Choices

Some people fear being overwhelmed by technology. Cars. Computers. Cell phones. Coffee makers. Are we helpless in the face of this onslaught of new products?

"Our worst nightmare is that we will fall victim to our technologies," says Paul Saffo, a director at the Institute for the Future in Menlo Park, California. "In fact the technologies remain firmly under our control."

- Betsey Moses, a high school teacher, decided not to get a telephone answering machine. "It would create more for me to do."
- Cynthia and David Ott, computer chip designers, decided not to own or drive a car.
- One mother won't allow cable TV into her home because it would take up precious time."
- Dr. Steve Crandall still uses a slide rule.

We can decide for ourselves if a particular piece of technology is a help or a hindrance.

Decide with equity. (Isaiah 11:4)

Father, help us to make wise choices.

His Life Is Not His Own

Dominique Lapierre spends most of his time with lepers and the poor in India. He is a writer who has been drawn to the places that inspired his books, *Freedom at Midnight* and *City of Joy.*

Lapierre has spent two decades and $5 million from book royalties on small unpublicized projects to help the desperately needy people he has come to know and love.

Problems are vast. Distrusting bureaucracies and official forms of aid, the author cites problems of waste and corruption. He tries to provide the basics that so many of us take for granted, such as doctors and medicine, teachers and education.

Lapierre calls poor people "the real heroes of the planet."

What can you do today to be a hero to someone in serious need?

Blessed are the merciful, for they will receive mercy. (Matthew 5:7)

Spirit, enable me to see Jesus in the the poor.

No More Bad Prayer Days

For those who have had difficulty praying, prayer is something for mystics and monks. But here are some tips to help end those "bad prayer" days.

- Throw away the script and talk with God person to Person about your worries and concerns; your joys and sorrows; your dreams and hopes; your loves and hates.

- Pray by listening; just sitting silently in God's presence in a church, your favorite chair, on the back porch, patio or balcony, in the car.

- Pray your distractions by making tomorrow's busy schedule or the results of a medical test the subject of prayer. Our business is God's business.

- Keep asking, acknowledging that there is very little in our lives that we can control on our own.

Just do it. Pray. Pray today. Now. Right where you are.

"Lord teach us to pray." (Luke 11:1)

Lord, hear my prayer.

New York's New Angle: Fishing

When most of us think of the nation's great fishing spots, it's a fair guess that the Bronx, New York, isn't likely one of them.

Yet, thanks to a consistent cleanup effort, the city's waters are teeming with fish and the anglers who seek them.

A startling number of striped bass migrated up the Hudson River one recent spring, according to *Time Out New York* magazine. Authorities, who are anticipating a return of the days when nets hauled in stripers, cod, blues, shad and lobster, are considering allowing commercial fishing once again. And fishing has regained its spot among New Yorkers' favorite outdoor sport.

Rebirth can happen in the most unlikely places. Don't give up on your efforts to improve something–whatever it may be or however hopeless it may seem. You may be surprised at the outcome.

Cast your net to the right side of the boat, and you will find some. (John 21:6)

Dear God, bless this world with surprises and happy endings every day.

Honoring the Common People

The pride of the Quito (Equador) Historic Center project, the Quito City Museum shows dioramas and artifacts ranging over the past four centuries from colonial sculptures, to Amazonian trees, to a 19th century horse carriage, to the huge kettles used for cooking on haciendas.

Half of those who visit the museum daily are school children learning about their past. As Museum Director Patricia von Buchwald says, "People with knowledge of their past have high self-esteem. They know that they can do, what they set out to do. ...we are all builders, not just the heroes and great artists. This museum pays homage to the anonymous builders of the city."

Honoring our past allows us to better understand the present and to embrace the future with hope and confidence. Take time out to learn about and honor the forgotten men and women who were an integral part of your own community's history.

(Proclaim) liberty to one another. (Jeremiah 34:15)

Through mutual respect may we give one another the freedom to develop, Father-Creator.

The Perfect Schedule

Baseball is a game of numbers that appeals to mathematicians. Batting averages, earned runs allowed, the minutiae of the game are predicated on mathematical formulas.

There's the challenge of scheduling Major League Baseball games: the two leagues, each with three divisions; a total of 30 teams playing 162 games a year!

Getting the season's schedule right can be a nightmare, but not to Holly and Henry Stephenson. Working out of a 2nd floor office in their Victorian home for more than 17 years, they've done the seemingly impossible. But, "even after you figure it out, there are special requests," says Henry Stephenson.

The Stephensons have been able to do what scientists at Georgia Tech and Stanford have not– build a superior system of scheduling for a $2.5 billion industry.

Use your God-given intelligence diligently.

Bless your Maker, who fills you with His good gifts. (Sirach 32:13)

Lord God, thank you for the ability to reason, to solve problems, to weigh and decide.

Remembering to Remember

Time magazine columnist Amy Dickinson looks forward to Memorial Day each year. She regards the traditional start of summer as the time "when kids start dreaming in color again," and she makes an effort to plant flowers, wash the porch, and savor a family barbecue.

"But for us, the best thing about the holiday is the part that has become an afterthought for many people," she writes, "the remembering."

Dickinson points to Memorial Day as a great opportunity for families to bond. She urges parents to explain the holiday to their children, and to visit their local war memorial.

She suggests using the day to share family stories and photo albums.

"Before you stoke up the grill this year," she concludes, "raise a glass to the people who came before you—those who fought for our country or tended the home fires—and help your family celebrate its past."

Remember the deeds of the ancestors. (1 Maccabees 2:51)

Thank you, Lord, for those who have sacrificed that we may live in freedom.

Give my Regards to Broadway

Alix Strauss culled the wisdom of show business for a "words to live by" feature in *Family Circle* magazine. The sayings provide inspiration worth considering when the going gets tough.

Feeling unappreciated or unable to find the recognition you deserve? "There are no bit parts."

Overworked? Determined to take on more responsibility than may be necessary? Unwilling to delegate? "Everyone should have an understudy," says Strauss, and "sometimes we need...an intermission."

Those who are trying to jumpstart the next phase of their lives may benefit by her suggestion to "change your scenery," or find encouragement in her advice to "stick around because the second act may surprise you."

Whatever dreams you are pursuing or hopes you have for the future, "give it all you've got" and "smile, smile, smile!"

Hope for good things. (Sirach 2:9)

Lord God, let us cherish the roles You have given us, and shine with Your love.

Legionnaire Extraordinaire

"There's going to be a very special place in heaven for the likes of Annie Dickson." That's what the president of the Fair Lawn Veteran's Council has to say about New Jersey Veterans Memorial Home volunteer Ann Dickson, a spry 78-year-old widow, grandmother and World War II Army Auxiliary Corps veteran. The reason? Dickson gives of herself completely and enthusiastically to help relieve the oftentimes numbing sameness of institutional life for our veterans.

For her part, the former Army medical assistant gets peace of mind from her various duties-from running bingo games to dropping off donations to organizing parties. She feels that the residents "get something they probably wouldn't get if I hadn't stepped in." Best of all, people weakened by age, disease and loneliness gain her friendship.

People like Ann Dickson embody the impulse to reach out and lend a helping hand or ear. Make volunteerism a lifelong habit. The rewards are immeasurable.

Work for the good of all. (Galatians 6:10)

Master, teach me to be generous with my time and talents.

Has America Forgotten Its Spanish Roots?

England was America's mother country. Right? Well, yes, but, "Spain was also a mother country," notes Thomas E. Chavez. A 13th generation resident of Santa Fe, N.M., he is director of the museum at the Palace of the Governors in Santa Fe. Built in 1610, it is the oldest government building in the U.S.

National publicity was sparse during the 400th anniversary of the 1598 crossing of the Rio Grande by Don Juan de Oñate and 500 colonists, much to the annoyance of Hispanic participants.

Yet, the celebration of Don Juan de Oñate's 1598 trek did seem to lead to some reconciliation in the centuries-long conflict between Native Americans and Spain over past violence.

The United States owes its existence to the sacrifices and contributions of many.

To make this nation work for the common good today, mutual respect is vital.

Whose offspring are worthy of honor? Those who fear the Lord. (Sirach 10:19)

Father, teach us how to respect one another.

Thanks a Million

Each week, millionaire Percy Ross reaches out through his newspaper column to a handful of the thousands of people who write to him. They ask for a few hundred dollars to help them through a crisis, find a new start, or pay a past debt that keeps them from moving on. Ross responds most openly to those who are actively seeking ways to improve themselves.

Once he devoted an entire column to explaining why he has chosen to give away his wealth during his lifetime.

While working as an auctioneer, he saw first-hand that all possessions are only temporarily owned. "They are loaned to us for our brief enjoyment and enrichment," he wrote, but "the time will come when they will belong to others." He believes that the love and respect of others is the only possession we can take to the grave with us.

Ross hopes that those whom he helps will, in turn, remember to help others when they can.

One's life does not consist in the abundance of possessions. (Luke 12:15)

God, help us to both give and receive according to Your will.

Get More Out of Life

It seems likely that the more you put into life, the more you'll get out of it. But when it comes to the rewards of physical activity, a little bit goes a long way.

The benefits of physical activity are well known: improved mood, reduced risk of obesity, heart disease, stroke, osteoporosis and certain cancers. Even, you'll look and feel good!

How much is enough? One study of twins showed those who walked briskly for half an hour at least six times a month were 48% less likely to die prematurely than non-walkers.

The U.S. Department of Health and Human Services suggests 30 total minutes a day of such moderate activities as gardening, brisk walking or dancing.

Wherever in life where you need to improve, start small. But start.

Your body is a temple of the Holy Spirit...therefore glorify God in your body. (1 Corinthians 6:19,20)

Encourage us, Lord, to get moving.

What Have I Learned?

Here are some thoughts from that wise person "Anonymous."

All I can do is try to be a loveable person.

It's taking much longer than I thought it would to become the person I'd like to be.

Some people will never care no matter how much I do.

It takes years to develop trust; seconds to ruin it.

It's not what but *who* I have in my life that's important.

I shouldn't compare myself to others.

I am responsible for what I do, no matter how I feel.

It takes practice to learn to forgive.

Even when I have a right to be angry, I don't have a right to be cruel.

Maturity is learning from the experiences I've had, not how old I am.

Every day presents a new chance to learn. Make the most of it.

May (we) gain a wise heart. (Psalm 90:12)

Abide with me my whole life-long, Redeemer.

Coaching? Or Building Bridges?

When we think of the word "coach," images of sports teams come to mind.

Yet the word means one who instructs, directs or prompts another. They play an important part in organized sports, but coaches are found in all walks of life. A coach could be:

- A teacher who takes the time to listen.
- A clergyperson who explains the Scripture clearly and with humor.
- A co-worker who trains new hires.
- A neighbor who welcomes a new person on the block.
- Anyone in the public eye who sets an example of leadership.

Coaches have been said to be the ones who "build bridges" so that others may cross. When in your life have you had the enviable opportunity to coach another? What a gift to have the chance to help another accomplish his or her goals!

Listen to advice and accept instruction. (Proverbs 19:20)

Bless us with the character and strength, Lord.

Dream a Little Dream

Ever have one of those dreams in which you're being chased? How about flying high above the clouds? Or the one where you're immobilized? Many of us have wondered exactly where dreams come from.

According to Paul Meier, M.D., a Christian psychiatrist, and his partner, Robert Wise, Ph.D., "God can speak to us in our dreams or our daydreams."

The authors of *Windows of the Soul,* their book on dreams and the psyche, advise, "...be careful. If you do believe God is speaking to you through a dream, look at it through the Scripture, get other advice and pray."

Dreams may be one way God chooses to reveal His plan for you. Listening to Him requires listening for Him in all aspects of your life.

The Lord is good to...the soul that seeks Him. (Lamentations 3:25)

Show me how to better listen to You, Father.

A Better Way

"What am I doing wrong?" "Why can't he just behave?" These are two questions weary parents ask themselves as they struggle to raise their children and instill discipline.

If you feel like all you do is yell at your kids, Gary Chapman, a pastor and family life counselor offers some helpful alternatives.

Positive discipline means turning a child away from disobedience and in the right direction. Correcting with words and actions are ways in which we teach and guide.

If your child continues to be defiant, punishment in the context of unconditional love is in order. We need to discipline our children because we love them, not instead of loving them. No matter how many times your child breaks the same rule, don't love him or her conditionally.

God loves us no matter what we do, no matter how often we transgress. Discipline your kids with that same kind of love.

Train children in the right way. (Proverbs 22:6)

God, help me to love unconditionally.

Finding a Wedding Ring in the Garbage

One evening, Daniel Carey lost his wedding ring in the trash. "That ring was the symbol of a vital turning point in my life," Carey explains.

His wife, Mary, had placed the ring on his finger in 1978, ten years after they had married. "Our marriage didn't make me settle down," Carey explains, "nor did the birth of our daughter. I kept drinking and smoking and carousing up a storm."

But coming home to an empty home one evening, his wife and daughter gone, did make Carey take notice. "I looked in the mirror and did not like what I saw," he recalls. "I prayed to God for the strength to change."

By 1978, Carey and his wife were together again. The ring was a symbol of that.

What happened to it? With a little help from a garbage truck driver and a lot of digging through trash, Carey found the gold nugget wedding ring gleaming inside a crushed egg carton, a shining reminder that everything in life worth having demands perseverance.

Happy are they who persevere. (Daniel 12:12)

Master, You hold the plan for my life. Help me to follow where You lead.

Opening Doors to a Future

InRoads is a national program that places talented minority students in corporate summer jobs. Started by publishing executive Frank Carr in 1970, the program boasts a roster of 6200 active interns, more than 900 corporate clients, and 7000 alumni nationwide.

More than a credit on a resume, the program stresses academics and social responsibility year 'round. Emphasis on leadership and community service is part of InRoads' appeal to the students and companies who benefit from the program.

As one corporate manager puts it, "InRoaders are willing to take on anything you ask...they've learned to get something out of every job experience."

Here is real hope for a fine future for a portion of America's youth–a sure cause for optimism within the corporate culture and the culture at large.

There is hope for a tree, if it is cut down, that it will sprout again. (Job 14:7)

Holy Spirit, help me to capitalize on my opportunities.

Swaddled in Love

Remember Linus from the popular *Peanuts* comic strip? He's the little one who felt safest when he was clutching his favorite blanket.

In 1995 Karen Loucks-Baker of Colorado read about a young girl with cancer whose security blanket helped her cope. She decided to begin providing homemade security blankets to the Rocky Mountain Children's Cancer Center in Denver. And that was the beginning of the now nation-wide "Project Linus."

We can provide comfort and a sense of security to a child through kind words, reading a favorite story, or simply listening.

Look to Jesus' example of caring for the little ones in His flock. Then ask yourself how you can help a young person near you.

Let the little children come to Me...(Jesus) took them up in His arms, laid His hands on them, and blessed them. (Mark 10:14,16)

Jesus, You welcomed children and the defenseless. Inspire my own efforts for them.

Sometimes, It Takes Two

With a name like Ocean Robbins, it's seems logical that he's an environmental activist.

Yet, it was a late night discussion with one of his summer campmates eight years ago that sparked the founding of YES! (Youth for Environmental Sanity), a non-profit environmental organization.

Since then, Ocean and his friend, co-founder Ryan Eliason have reached more than 500,000 students in 1200 schools nationwide with a single message: Take action to help preserve the environment.

Often our talents are best realized through a partnership. Whether it's in business, in a friendship or in marriage, the right partner can help us make a difference.

It is required of stewards that they be found trustworthy. (1 Corinthians 4:2)

Father, remind me that no one is an island; we need one another's company to be fully human.

Rey's Dream

It's a familiar story: parents have dreams for their youngsters and encourage them to dream.

Though Rey Ramos' parents spoke little English, they wanted their only son to have every opportunity. They enrolled him in a Head Start program. Then they saved enough for him to take music lessons. When he began acting up in junior high, they met with the principal.

Ramos' math and science teachers discovered his outstanding problem-solving abilities. And he started to think about becoming a doctor because he didn't like the way his mother had been treated at a local medical clinic.

Rey Ramos graduated from Harvard University in 1997 and decided to remain there to earn his medical degree. His dream: To open his own South Bronx clinic.

Parents, support your children's dreams and keep dreaming yourself.

Do to others as you would have them do to you; for this is the Law and the Prophets. (Matthew 7:12)

Inspire us, God, to believe we can overcome any obstacle.

Make a Pact with Yourself

Researchers have found that 30 to 45 percent of the nation's population is struggling with feelings of depression at any given time.

Psychologist Ellen McGrath has identified sixteen different kinds of the blues in her book, *The Complete Idiot's Guide to Beating the Blues.*

She also teaches that "It's important to hold the ordinary blues in check," McGrath explains, "because they can sometimes turn into" clinical depression which can make it difficult for people to function.

McGrath devised PACT (people, action, creativity, and time) to help her readers cope with the "ordinary blues."

Simply put, she suggests developing a network of people for support, staying healthy through activity, finding meaningful creativity, and allowing time to pass rather than turning to self-destructive behaviors such as overeating.

Not feeling 100 percent today? Use PACT to help you in your journey to a brighter day.

Cast your burden on the Lord, and He will sustain you. (Psalm 55:22)

God, give us strength to reflect Your love each day.

Not Just For Kids

If you think tree houses are just for kids, you haven't read Peter Nelson's book *Tree Houses: The Art and Craft of Living Out on a Limb* (Houghton Mifflin). It brought tree-house enthusiasts together because there is a whole community of adults who delight in life at the top.

The thirty something Nelson lives in a regular house with his wife and children. But to get to his office, this building contractor climbs a tree. A tree believer, he's convinced that "no good person doesn't like them." Of the arboreal houses he's seen or built, he says, "they're magical little structures."

It's serious business with rules about picking the right trees and building carefully to protect the health of the tree. And there's the World Treehouse Association in Oregon. But mostly it's fun.

Tree houses are used as overnight campsites; places of prayerful retreat; year-round "shacks"; offices and studios; adult hideaways. Oh, and kids seem to enjoy them too.

Unless the Lord builds the house, those who build it labor in vain. (Psalm 127:1)

Thank you, Lord, for the delights of nature.

It's All in the Timing

Composer Irving Berlin's daughter, Mary Ellin Barrett, remembers the first time her father sang *God Bless America* to her. "It was very touching," she told Newsday reporter Erik Holm. "The lyric...says, 'Land that I love.' It came from the heart when he sang it."

Berlin had emigrated to the United States from Russia with his parents when he was five. Struggling to capture the national mood just prior to WWII, Berlin wrote a song called *Thanks America*. When it didn't seem to work, he remembered another he had written as an Army sergeant in 1918.

A few weeks later, Kate Smith introduced the public to *God Bless America* at the end of her Armistice Day radio program.

Berlin wrote nearly 1,000 songs during his lifetime. "But," concluded Holm, "none would be more enduring than the song some people wanted to make the national anthem."

Let justice roll down like waters, and righteousness like an everflowing stream. (Amos 5:24)

Thank you for the beauty and the bounty of this land, Lord.

Alone Doesn't Equal Lonely

Approximately one-quarter of American households are comprised of people who live alone. Some are just beginning their adult lives. Some have chosen not to marry. Still others are single after being divorced or widowed.

Many people find being single comfortable and enjoyable. For those who find it takes work, Patricia Fry suggests:

- Accept your situation.
- Allow people to be part of your life.
- Reach out to others as a friend.
- Embrace the present.
- Get to know yourself as an individual.
- Invite God to walk with you.

Fry also points to author Mary Lewis Coakley who recommends putting "love into our lives by being loving."

My Lord...help me, who am alone. (Esther 14:3)

No matter what our situation in life, Dear Companion, help us build communities of love.

The Secrets of a Blissful Marriage

The couple that prays together stays together, or so it seems. Every morning at breakfast, Lee and Irene Carroll, married for over 60 years, have what they call quiet time. Some days they might read a Bible passage; other days they laugh about a funny story, or discuss a problem. But they spend at least 15 or 20 minutes being silent together. For the two, both in their nineties, quiet time is sacred time, during which they connect with each other and with God.

The Carrolls were once involved in a movement called the Oxford Group, whose goal was to help couples find deeper love and closeness to God in their marriages. This idea lives on in the movement known as Marriage Encounter.

Listen with your heart; learn how to describe feelings; write daily letters to each other—these keep a marriage fresh and vital, the Carrolls suggest. The key to a successful marriage? Says Irene Carroll, "you have to keep working on it every single day."

Let marriage be held in honor by all.
(Hebrews 13:4)

Lord of love, may marriages thrive through Your guidance.

When Rev. Father Is a Father

When Alec and John see Doug Cunningham, they see a father. So do Rev. Cunningham's Catholic parishioners.

His roles as priest and single parent enhance and enrich one another.

Rev. Cunningham adopted Alexander Douglas Liang Zi Wang and Donald John (DJ) Xi Xiong, from the same Chinese orphanage so they'd have that common bond.

The three are establishing new bonds as a family. Raising youngsters solo is always a challenge. Rev. Cunningham relies on the support of his parish family to help him.

But then there are the rewards: "Coming home at the end of the day and having someone to share the day with...is wonderful."

It is wonderful to be part of a family—whether one you've begun with another person or one formed in your house of worship, or both. Pray for all the families to which you belong.

Set the believers an example in speech and conduct. (1 Timothy 4:12)

Creator, bless all families.

The Children's Crusade

Whether in a crowded city or isolating sub-urb, life can be dangerous and forbidding for children. Where, for example, can they play?

Barbara Barlow, M.D., for example, was appalled at the lack of safe playgrounds for children in the Harlem area of New York. Vast tracks of asphalt or concrete were all that were available. Playgrounds had been usurped by drug addicts and traffickers, rats, and litter.

With single minded determination she cajoled a $125,000 grant and founded the Harlem Hospital Injury Prevention Program. Bright, clean, colorful, safe playgrounds (costing $60,000 each) resulted.

More and more benefactors are being attracted to this program.

Dr. Barlow has never taken a salary; her reward is the children's laughter.

Helping children always brings rewards.

Often have I desired to gather your children together as a hen gathers her brood under her wings. (Luke 13:34)

Give me, O Lord, the heart of a child that I may play in Your presence forever.

Why Bother with Ornamentation?

Cool. Functional. Sensible. Sleek. Are these traits the essence of modernity? Does 21st century architecture, for instance, require anything beyond geometric shapes? Pure rationality?

What about embellishment? Ornamentation? Some people believe that to adorn a building or other object is a token of esteem, even an act of love.

Perhaps it's true that we adorn and decorate that which we honor. If so, then even a quick look around might indicate that we don't think too highly of our buildings.

Stripped of ornament, our cities are stripped of soul. It may be time to right the balance. Time to build things we love and to love our creations.

"Architecture began as a ritual of celebration," writes Alvin Holm in the Philadelphia Inquirer, "and must continue in that spirit if we are to enter the 21st century with honor and grace."

The smith, sitting by the anvil, intent on his iron-work...is careful to complete its decoration. (Sirach 38:28)

God, help us to appreciate beauty in its many guises.

Think before Speaking

Think before you speak," is good advice for people of every age.

While discussing the purchase of a gift a teenage girl said to her parents, "I have a better suggestion."

Her father quickly corrected her, "You have a different suggestion, you don't know that it is better."

When her father saw her puzzled expression he explained, "We your parents love you, understand you and know you. We know what you meant. Using the word 'better' as you did is tactless.

"The right choice of words will allow people to like you. Think about how your words will be heard or understood by others."

Silence is golden. Tact is platinum.

A word fitly spoken is like apples of gold in a setting of silver. (Proverbs 25:11)

Jesus, teach me to think of others' feelings.

Words of Encouragement

The June morning of her friend's father's funeral, Gerri Meade told her friend, "Remember ...his soul is with God." The friend's cousin who was in the same room heard what Gerri said. The cousin thought, "What a wonderful phrase, I hope I can remember it. I know those words of consolation will be of help."

On a late June afternoon, seven years later, the cousin walked into the hospital room where her deceased mother lay. Simultaneously with the onset of tears came the thought, "my mother is with God."

When the cousin wrote acknowledging the Mass Card, she told Meade of her compassionate words, and how they were of consolation seven years later.

Often a word of encouragement to one person at a specific time later touches the mind and heart of another.

The lips of many tell of their good sense. (Sirach 2:24)

Lord God, teach us how to encourage and console wisely.

Adjusting to Change

"It won't be like the world is coming to an end," said Steven W. Blamer, chief executive of Grey Advertising in London. "But we're going to have to deal with it."

He is talking about change—disruptive, necessary, inevitable, even positive. He was referring to Britain's changing the initial digits of just about all telephones in the country. Called the city code, it is similar to a U.S. area code.

Establishing the new codes affects existing phone system software, business cards, letterhead stationery and billboards.

Codes must be changed because of the unanticipated use of cell phones, Internet lines and fax machines and the resulting need for new phone numbers.

Despite the price that must be paid to accommodate the requirements of the new technology, some feel it's worth it because life will be improved. That's debatable. What can't be argued is that change is part of life. And we need strategies to cope with it.

I the Lord do not change. (Malachi 3:6)

Help us, Lord, to manage change wisely.

Fragile: Reprimand with Care

Two women talking about their childhoods, each described her mother's reprimands.

One mother scolded, "Don't talk back to me. It is bad." The child thought about this and asked, "Am I a bad girl?" Her mother immediately said, "You have bad manners, you are not bad. You are a fresh little girl."

The other woman's mother daily rebuked, "Stop putting your feet on the rungs of the chair. Stop this bad habit." To stress her displeasure she added, "You are a bold child."

Both mothers separated the individual from the action when reprimanding their daughters. Each daughter understood without a doubt that her mother loved her, but not her behavior.

When correcting our children let us choose our words as carefully as those mothers did.

Like...an ornament of gold is a wise rebuke to a listening ear. (Proverbs 25:12)

El Shaddai, help me always to remember that words can hurt or they can heal.

A Family Member

Lu Zhi, a zoologist and a leader of China's nascent conservation movement, may know more than anyone else about China's giant panda.

When Lu Zhi started her research, little was known about them and their habits. Playing down the hardships, she spent most of seven years tracking them in the wild. She came to know pandas "like members of a family." And she found that if left alone in their mountain-fastness they'll thrive just fine.

To protect their isolation Lu Zhi has worked to harmonize the needs of pandas with the economic development of poor farmers.

It's important to balance our needs with the conservation and preservation of natural habitats for wildlife. Animals are, after all, integral to our physical and mental health and that of the earth.

Give me an accounting of your management. (Luke 16:2)

Bless and protect the beasts, kind Lord.

Recharging Your Batteries

Want to know a little secret about how to liven up your life, rekindle energy, and brighten your outlook? Take a little vacation every day.

You don't have to go to the mountains to ski, or the beach to swim, you simply have to spend some time each day doing something you really love. If you like to read, keep a book handy and lose yourself in an author you really like. If you like to sketch, keep a pad and pencil handy. The idea is to focus your full attention on this pleasurable activity.

It is very difficult for many of us to take time from our busy schedules for a typical vacation. But, if we took just 15 minutes from every day, that's 91 hours a year, or two full weeks!

And what are we doing? Something we love. That is exhilarating, refreshing, revivifying. And that is what a vacation is supposed to do.

"Come away to a deserted place all by your-selves and rest a while." (Mark 6:31)

Take Me, O Lord, in my quiet moments into the radiance of Your Presence.

Left Out

Writing in *Guideposts* magazine, one woman tells how left out she felt when–despite the fact that he'd been so important in her life–she wasn't invited to her cousin's wedding.

The woman had loved and supported the groom-to-be, actually her first cousin's son, ever since his birth. In her mind he was the child she could never have. She had doted on her little cousin.

While the writer understood the practical reasons for not being invited to the young man's wedding (a large extended family and not enough money to invite them all), she still was hurt. She felt she'd had a special relationship with him. She'd even made plane reservations for the trip and sent an expensive gift.

"But I realized there was something more I wanted to give to the bride and groom: peace, love, happiness. Not my hurt feelings. Not a family torn by anger and gossip."

Bless your Maker, who fills you with His good gifts. (Sirach 32:13)

When I'm tempted to self-pity, God, deliver me.

Retirement: Time of Increased Activity

Retirement is not a time to spend just watching the rest of life go by.

It is a time of renewal, a time to reassess our spiritual direction and begin anew. Until retirement, much of our attention had to be directed toward making a living, providing for our later years. With that burden diminished, we can focus not on what we do, but who we are.

We can use the same tools we have used all along: spiritual reading, meditation, prayer, the sacraments, Mass, and retreats.

We can...

1) Redefine ourselves. 2) Reframe our attitudes to ones of spiritual adventure and growth. 3) Restructure our lives to our own personal goals.

Retirement is a chance to take the hunger for God to new and exciting levels, to give life a richer meaning.

In the morning sow...and at evening do not...be idle. (Ecclesiastes 11:6)

Help me to realize, God, that life is a gift at every age.

Building Peace at Home

Too many of us feel numbed and helpless about the violence destroying the lives of young people in their schools. What can done?

The Hamilton Township, New Jersey school district has a Peacemaking Project. Every day students recite "A Pledge for Peace." It reads, in part, "I pledge to be a peaceful person...in my school, with my family, my community. I pledge not to fight with others. I pledge to make my world a more peaceful place for children to be safe, happy and peaceful. I pledge to set a peaceful example."

Youngsters are also taught conflict resolution: Cool off. State feeling through "I" messages. No blaming. No name calling. No interrupting. State the problem as the other person sees it. Express personal responsibility. Brainstorm solutions to satisfy both. Affirm, forgive or thank the other person.

If we do not accept that peace begins and ends with each individual, we will never have a peaceful world.

A harvest of righteousness is sown in peace for those who make peace. (James 3:18)

Spirit of Peace, help me to follow You even when it is hard to love and easy to hate.

The Hat that Launched a Company

In 1979, Heida Thurlow, president of Chantal Cookware, traveled to a Chicago trade show hoping to put her fledgling company on the map. "The first day I had a small booth and not a single person stopped by," Thurlow recalls.

Realizing that she did not have the name or company size to get noticed, she tried a different approach. On the second day of the trade show, Thurlow showed up wearing an outrageous hat. "Everyone stopped by to comment on it," Thurlow says, "and I would say, 'Well, how about looking at my roasters, too?'"

Her strategy worked, winning her an order for several hundred pieces and the break she needed. Today her company is a leading maker of enamel-on-steel cookware.

Thurlow says, "Success often takes longer than you expect. Believe in yourself. Take a calculated risk. Stop waiting for someone else to do it for you."

Wisdom helps one to succeed.
(Ecclesiastes 10:10)

May my every action and word lead others to You, Lord.

Caring for One Another

Sixteen-year-old John arrived in the United States, his adopted country, in June of 1911.

He got a job working 12-hour days. Some days were split shifts—six hours on, six off, and six on again. When he could, John went to school to learn to speak, read and write English.

John was introduced to a couple with whom he boarded for several years. Their children were just about his own age.

Within the first year of his arrival, John caught the measles and was very sick. The doctor wanted to put him in quarantine.

But the couple with whom he lived refused, saying that he would never survive. They added that he was "alone and has no one here" and promised "we will care for him as we did our own children." And they did.

That couple had great kindness and insight. Do we extend ourselves to those who need a helping hand?

The Lord has compassion...He remembers that we are dust. (Psalm 103:13,14)

Spirit of Love, help us be compassionate.

To Build a Sand Castle

Here are the basics of sand castle construction: Fill a five-gallon plastic pail half-way with water. Add fine-grained silty sand to just below the water line. Maintain this sloppy mix throughout construction.

Using both hands, scoop out sand and mold it into bricks. Shake out excess water. Lay bricks end to end to form each wall.

Flatten other double handfuls into pancakes and use these to form the tower(s). Be sure the tower narrows as it goes up.

Using a broken-tip plastic knife and a small paintbrush, and working from the top down, add details: windows, exterior staircase.

Stand back, admire your castle. And water it every half-hour.

For life itself, sound building and regular maintenance are a must. Tend the life God's given you today.

Someone...who comes to Me, hears My words, and acts on them...is like a man building a house, who...laid the foundation on rock. (Luke 6:47,48)

Open my ears, my mind and my heart to Your wisdom, Jesus. Then, help me act on it.

Lessons from Feeding the Ducks

Jacqueline Tresl always considered her grandfather her best friend. "He taught me how to dig ginseng in the woods around our home. He rigged-up treasure hunts with elaborate clues leading to a new Kennedy half-dollar."

Tresl's grandfather also taught her about life. Tresl would regularly visit the cemetery with her grandfather and grandmother to weed the graves.

The first hour of each visit was spent feeding the ducks at the pond. "When I asked what the ducks do in winter when people weren't there to leave them bread, granddad would tell me that these ducks had short life spans," Tresl recalls, "that many of them would be gone when we returned."

Tresl continued: "Granddad prepared me for the day I'd visit the cemetery without him. He taught me life is short and saw to it that we never wasted a minute of our time together."

The race is not to the swift...nor bread to the wise, nor riches to the intelligent, nor favor to the skillful; but time and chance happen to them all. (Ecclesiastes 9:11)

Help me, Father, to remember the great gifts You have given me.

Time for Courtesy

Courtesy has been described as the lubricant that eases the friction arising from differences among human beings. By setting accepted limits on what people may say or do to one another, it prevents those differences from igniting strife.

Here are some more thoughts:

"Courtesy is the one passport that will be accepted without question in every land, in every office, in every home, in every heart in the world. For nothing commends itself so well as kindness: and courtesy is kindness."–George Powers

"Courtesy is the best part of culture, a kind of enchantment that wins the good will of all."

–Baltasar Gracian

"What is courtesy? It is the beginning of friendship. It is the beginning of an open mind, when you realize that all people are children of God and that they deserve the same consideration and treatment that you expect."

–Maxwell Maltz

Civility and courtesy are as necessary today as ever.

Show every courtesy to everyone. (Titus 3:2)

Show me how to reflect Your own gracious courtesy in all I do, Lord God.

Snap, Crackle, Boom!

Each year at Independence Day, many Americans look to one event that truly signals the holiday's significance: fireworks.

However American fireworks may be linked to our history today, did you know how and where they were actually developed?

Alchemists in medieval China experimented with purified chemicals in search of an "elixir of life." Around 850 AD, they tried combining saltpeter with charcoal and sulfur. The result was startling and eventually known as gunpowder. The rest is history.

One of the many beautiful things about America is that it is inherently diverse; its culture an amalgam of many cultures. Even our history is inextricably linked to those of other nations. Take pride in the fact that America has been built on the coming together of people from everywhere else.

You were called to freedom...only do not use your freedom as an opportunity for self-indulgence. (Galatians 5:13)

Help me appreciate, Father, the rich diversity of my country.

Summer Reading for Little Ones

Some youngsters take to reading almost as naturally as breathing and it is hard to pry a book out of their hands. Others need motivation, especially when school lets out.

Beth Oliver and Vicky Bentley of Phoenix, Arizona, decided to encourage their children by forming a neighborhood book club. Their goal: each child reads at least five hours a week. Each child designs a poster to track hours and books read. "At club meetings, the children present their posters" and give brief book reports. The rewards: bowling, swimming or the movies.

"It's been a fun, easy way to keep our children reading without argument and looking forward to getting together. They're as proud of their achievements as we are."

Youngsters need to set goals and achieve them, just as adults do. It is a key to developing a good sense of self-worth.

I press on to make (the goal) my own, because Christ Jesus has made me His own. (Philippians 3:12)

Jesus, guide my efforts to accomplish my goals.

The First Tourists

If tourism strikes you as being relatively recent in human experience, that's not the case. Admittedly, until fairly modern times it was reserved for wealthy people. Still, two thousand years ago, Romans started to become overseas sightseers.

The Pax Romana, insured by the Empire's army and navy, was a period relatively free from war. Citizens took advantage of this safety to book deck passage on freighters. Their destinations were places famous in history and legend.

Intrigued by the glories of ancient Greece, visitors wanted to see sites mentioned in Homer's *Odyssey* and *Iliad*. In Egypt, they sought out the Sphinx, the Pyramids and the Valley of the Kings—just as tourists do today. And they bought souvenirs.

Sometimes it seems that there is nothing new under the sun. Yet, when seen with fresh eyes, we can gain insight. Keep your eyes open to all around you.

Look up and see! (Isaiah 42:18)

Show me how to appreciate and learn from every experience Lord.

Growth—For Teenagers and Their Crops

Young participants in The Food Project of Boston are learning lessons about farming and about life.

The Food Project is a summer program for a diverse array of teenagers which pays them to grow vegetables later sold at farmers markets, donated to food pantries and served at shelters.

Each year 50 youngsters are selected from about 150 applicants. The careful mix deliberately includes 55-60% city residents and the rest suburbanites.

Teens either work on the Food Project's farm or its city garden and learn about such necessities as preparing the soil for plants and vegetables, weeding, and insect control.

Perhaps more important, the youngsters learn how to communicate, cooperate, solve problems and make friends.

Give me understanding that I may live. (Psalm 119:144)

Instruct us, Almighty Father, in ways to plant seeds of harmony and community.

Caretaker for Creatures of the Sea

Not many people in Dalyan, Turkey were even aware of the wondrous spectacle that had been occurring on their beaches every summer for decades. Each night, dozens of loggerhead turtles, some more than 100 years old, emerge from the surf to lay their eggs in deep holes they dig in the sand. They then return to the sea.

British-born June Haimoff had been watching the turtles for years when she learned of a developer's plans to erect a massive hotel complex on the beach.

Aware that the development would interfere with and most likely endanger the turtles' existence, Haimoff took action. Through her efforts, an international campaign to help keep the turtles' beach safe for breeding was begun.

It's hard to remain committed to something in the face of adversity. Yet that is the commitment that is most necessary. The greater the odds, the more glorious the victory.

The one who endures to the end will be saved. (Matthew 10:22)

Jesus, remind me of Your victory over death whenever my perseverance wavers.

Come to Jamaica and Feel...Blessed

Rev. Richard Ho Lung, with the Missionaries of the Poor, ministers to people of all ages with physical and mental disabilities, in Kingston, Jamaica.

While few give them a second thought, Rev. Ho Lung tells outsiders their story. He challenged Long Island, New York, parishioners to come to Jamaica for a brief mission immersion experience of feeding, bathing and otherwise tending to daily needs.

"Sign up now, don't worry about...how you'll pay," he pitched with abandon. "The Holy Spirit will take care of the rest."

Some of the Long Islanders initially felt uncomfortable in the midst of the severe disabilities they saw. But they soon appreciated the way these people were facing their challenges. One visitor said that she found the work as demanding as it was rewarding.

By the end of the trip, they all felt blessed by the experience.

**I was sick and you took care of me.
(Matthew 25:36)**

Teach us how to care for one another, Jesus.

Keepers of the River

In 1966, Hudson River commercial fishermen remembered how the river had teemed with striped bass, bluefish, giant sturgeon and herring. They knew cities were carelessly releasing millions of gallons of sewage into the river each day and that industries dumped chemicals, paint, and oil.

They formed an association and used the Refuse Act of 1899, written to make the polluting of American waters illegal, to "prosecute the polluters one at a time." Two years later they used a lawsuit to shut down a violator.

Today Robert F. Kennedy, Jr. serves as chief prosecuting attorney for the group's offshoot, Riverkeepers, Inc. In an article for *Life* he wrote that now "the Hudson produces more fish per acre than most other major estuaries of the North Atlantic. Boaters, swimmers, fish and fishermen have returned to the river."

What can you do each day to protect the waterways in your region, state, country?

I give water in the wilderness, rivers in the desert. (Isaiah 43:20)

May we be good stewards of all the earth's precious resources, Creator and Redeemer.

The Sweetness of Friendship

When Marshall Dean and Bobby Roth were growing up a friendly rivalry showed itself in a game of marbles. One day, after Bobby had taken all of Marshall's marbles, Marshall told his mom. Bobby called his friend a "dirty snitch and a sore loser."

Later, after spotting an announcement for a citywide marbles tournament, Marshall decided to talk Bobby into entering, figuring someone would beat him for sure and show him how it felt.

Bobby proceeded to mow down each opponent he faced. As the final match approached, Marshall came to realize he didn't want his friend to lose. After all, they were best friends. After Bobby won the tournament, he told a reporter, "I wouldn't have entered if my best buddy hadn't talked me into it."

Marshall learned a valuable lesson: revenge might be sweet but friendship is sweeter. Appreciate and cultivate your friends. They are invaluable.

Faithful friends are a sturdy shelter...a treasure. ...beyond price...life-saving medicine. (Sirach 6:14,15,16)

I cherish Your friendship and love, Christ Jesus.

In the Comfort of the Lord

It takes more than an intruder in the wee hours to shake up Mary Mack Brown, a wheelchair-bound octogenarian survivor of three cardiac arrests. She has always counted on God to help and protect her. So when the tall young man broke into the Charleston, South Carolina, home she'd lived in for almost 60 years and told her he was going to kill her, she remained calm.

She had said her evening prayers, then settled down to sleep "in the comfort of the Lord." When threatened she leaned on God.

She told the intruder, "You wouldn't want anyone doing this to your grandmother." When told he needed money for food, she suggested he help himself to food from her refrigerator. After taking nothing and apologizing to her, Brown said, "God sent you...Go...get some help."

Mary Mack Brown is an example of someone who trusts in God and lives her faith. We never know when each of us will be in a position to deliver a positive message of hope and salvation.

Blessed are those who trust in the Lord. (Jeremiah 17:7,8)

Lord, You hold my days and my nights in Your hands.

Summertime—and the Living Is Easy?

One morning, nine-year-old Ashley asked, "Mom, can I please be sick today? I just want to stay home and do nothing." Ashley was sending an SOS caused by SOS: Summer Overload Syndrome.

Summer *is* packed with activities. But it is important for the young to be free: to create, to think, to play quietly, to experience, to "be."

Consider these suggestions to make summertime living "easy" for the kids in your life:

- Choose only one big activity each month.
- Plan special activities each week, but allow several days between activities.
- Allow for creative time with "Summer Surprise Boxes" filled with either construction paper, markers, colored chalk, a glue stick and small scissor, or old clothes, hats and jewelry.
- Suggest that your child record thoughts and draw pictures during quiet times with God.

In...rest you shall be saved; in quietness and in trust shall be your strength. (Isaiah 30:16)

Slow me down, Lord. Help me find You in the stillness. Help me hear You in the silence.

Serenading the Whales

"Mostly what they get from us is a lot of engine noise, and that's certainly not the best human beings have to offer," said Fred West, speaking of the sounds traditionally heard by whales.

So West and the group he directs, Seattle's City Cantabile Choir, took to the waters around Washington's San Juan Islands to rectify this situation—at least for one summer evening. Out at sea, the group gave a concert for the whales.

The evening's program included a variety of music, from traditional religious songs—"Amazing Grace," to name one—to an eclectic mix of the sounds of various cultures.

And although there were no standing ovations or clapping of hands, about a dozen whales did show up—and stayed for the whole event.

"If we could just put aside that we're the top of the heap on this earth, we might just really learn something from other species," West offered.

Bless the Lord, you whales and all that swim in the waters. (Daniel 3:79)

Creator of all things, help me to live in harmony and in unity with all You have made.

Don't Tell Me What to Do!

Chicago newspaper columnist, Sydney J. Harris, once wrote a column about going to a newspaper stand with a friend.

The vendor was quite mean and shoved the paper at Harris' friend. The friend gave him the money and said, "Have a nice day, Charlie." To that the vendor replied, "Don't tell me what kind of day to have. I have other plans."

As they walked away, Harris said to his friend, "Is he always so mean? And are you're always so nice to him?" The friend answered: "Yes Why?"

"Well," Harris replied, "I was going to ask you why, if he's always so mean, you're always so nice to him." "Because," said Harris's friend, "I don't want him to decide how I'm going to act."

It is easy to be kind to those who are kind to us. The real test is to be kind to those not-so-inclined to return the attitude.

Love your enemies and pray for those who persecute you so that you may be children of your Father in heaven. (Matthew 5:44-45)

Lord, help me to mirror Your face to all I meet.

Breathing Life into the Dead Zone

Biologist Nancy Rabalais is literally trying to hold back the tide.

She is trying to save the coastal waters of the Gulf of Mexico. Through the years, as climatic conditions changed, a larger and larger area, some 8,000 square miles from Louisiana to the Texas border, has become a "dead zone."

No living thing can survive in the "dead zone," not crabs, shrimp, spade fish, bluefish, or triggerfish. Algae blooms from all of the fertilizers and pesticides prevent sunlight from penetrating below the water's surface. They deplete the water of the dissolved oxygen that marine life needs to survive.

In spite of her recent Blasker Award for Environmental Science and Engineering, Rabalais feels her work is just beginning. She has become an ambassador for a change that daily becomes more urgent.

God created the great sea. (Genesis 1:21)

Let your Spirit move in and through me, giving me Life.

The Eyes Have It

Why would a man with five children, a wife, and a flourishing business spend thirty hours a week doing more work? The answer is clear when you see the satisfaction on the face of Paul Berman.

Berman, an optometrist in Hackensack, New Jersey, helps participants in the Special Olympics. In 1989, Berman's program gave screenings and referrals to Special Olympians. In 1996, his organization began providing free eye-wear. In North Carolina his volunteers screened 1,500 athletes and gave away 800 pairs of glasses and protective goggles.

But figures cannot express the change in attitude and the flowering of the athletes. "Too often doctors overlook the vision problems of people with mental retardation. Special Olympic athletes deserve adequate eye care."

How can you use your expertise to help others?

We have gifts that differ according to the grace given. (Romans 12:6)

Help me, O Lord, to see Your face in all creation.

Turning a Myth into a Man

For almost three decades, Nelson Mandela was arguably the world's most famous political prisoner. During the long effort to transform South African apartheid into a democracy, he became a symbol, as well as a savior figure.

Yet as he argued, "I was not a messiah, but an ordinary man who had become a leader because of extraordinary circumstances." In other words, his story is of one man rising to the occasion as best he knew how.

Mandela always maintained he was willing to die in order to achieve his ideal of a democratic and open society, and today, as a world leader, he remains committed to that notion.

The road has not been easy, yet his integrity and character underscore his humanity, political and personal failings notwithstanding. Heroes are human, it's that simple.

If a new age of faith, hope and charity is attainable, it will be because we all practice forgiveness, sacrifice and humility.

The steadfast love of the Lord never ceases. (Lamentations 3:22)

Spirit, inspire me to realize my fullest humanity.

Trading Leisure for Charity

We working Americans crave our vacation time and guard it fiercely.

Sharon Bagalio, a registered nurse in Portland, Maine, also enjoyed time off. But upon seeing newspaper photos of ethnic Albanians suffering the effects of war, the mother of four youngsters decided to give up something that meant so much to her, her vacation time.

Bagalio was on a fixed budget, but since her hospital permitted employees to "cash in" unused vacation days, Bagalio did exactly that. What's more, she earned the hospital's support to encourage other employees to do the same. The result: Bagalio presented a check for $7,000 to the American Red Cross' Kosovo relief effort.

What can you give away to assist someone in need? Money isn't everything. Be creative and you could discover a new way to assist others.

The Lord Jesus...said, 'It is more blessed to give than to receive.' (Acts 20:35)

Father, remind me that it is my responsibility to provide for those in need.

On Promises Kept

The Vietnam War means different things to different people: a lesson in history books; a receding memory; an unforgettable life-changing event; a bracelet worn for a soldier who was a prisoner of war.

For Forrest, the Vietnam War was a story somehow linked to his mother's old POW bracelet and to the inscription: Capt. Byron Fuller, 7-14-67. "Everybody wore those back when I was a kid," Lisa Estes Ford told her son as they sorted through her old jewelry box.

Bracelet wearers prayed that "their" soldier would return home safely. After a time, Lisa Ford stored her bracelet in a jewelry box. Then one day her inquisitive son asked whatever happened to Capt. Fuller.

Following several unsuccessful attempts, she located former POW Fuller at home in the U.S. About his time in prison, he said, "I felt a lot of people praying for me."

Run with perseverance the race...before us. (Hebrews 12:1)

Lord, hear our prayers for those who guard the peace.

Scholar Honors His Mentor

Charles J. Ogletree Jr. plans to honor his mentor, another nationally known black legal scholar, by completing his unfinished books and articles.

"I love the man and have enormous respect for what he accomplished," said Professor Ogletree, about the late Leon Higginbotham Jr., a Federal appeals court judge. "I would do whatever he asked to complete his work."

Judge Higginbotham, the son of a laborer and a maid, fought poverty and bigotry to achieve his high position. He had definite ideas about how the system could be used to help others.

Professor Ogletree was also the son of a laborer and the first in his family to finish highschool. His goal in this project is to write in the voice of the man he calls a father figure.

Both men, Harvard Law School scholars, shared the belief that the legal system needs to continue the fight against assaults on civil rights.

What can you do to uphold the rights of others?

**Act with justice and righteousness.
(Jeremiah 22:3)**

Father, help struggle for justice.

That's What We're Here For

Going out isn't something Judi Chapman did much - partly because of her dependence on supplemental oxygen, partly because she's a writer. As a result, Chapman has a second "dependency": her computer.

One day her computer picked up a bug. A call to a local university's computer help line failed to fix the problem. Because Chapman didn't drive, the technician she spoke with volunteered to pick up an anti-virus program and bring it to her home. It meant going a half hour out of his way, after having spent two hours trying to help her on the phone.

Chapman met her Good Samaritan at the door of the apartment building where she lived. She offered him some money, but he refused. "We're here to help each other if we can," he told her.

Show kindness and mercy to one another. (Zechariah 7:9)

Help me, Lord, to help others this day.

Famous Ducks on the Water

Passengers seated on board one of the Original Wisconsin Duck vessels, probably may not realize they are on a "history" cruise.

More than 21,200 of these water vehicles, commonly referred to as Ducks, were manufactured between 1942 and 1945.

The Duck provided the army with a sophisticated transport vehicle that had enough marine capabilities to overcome rugged sea conditions. Its most famous military use was its participation in the historic D-Day invasion, June 6, 1944, at Normandy, France. Two thousand Ducks were used to transport soldiers and supplies from ship to shore. That surprise invasion of 155,000 Allied troops reclaimed nearly 80 square miles of France.

Duck tours began in Wisconsin in 1956. Today they have the largest fleet of Ducks in the United States, a total of 70. All those vehicles are named after famous military leaders of battles in which they participated.

Appreciate the history that surrounds you.

Our name will be forgotten in time.
(Wisdom of Solomon 2:4)

Help me to find You, Lord, in this day.

An Unconditional Apology

Mohandas K. Gandhi spent nearly twenty years in South Africa representing the interests of an Indian-based trading company. While in Johannesburg, Gandhi developed his philosophy of passive resistance and led countless human rights protest marches and strikes. He was imprisoned on several occasions.

Gandhi was the first non-white in South Africa to apply for legal credentials from the Natal Law Society, the equivalent of the bar association. The Society rejected his request to practice law because he was "not of European descent," but on appeal the country's chief justice admitted Gandhi to the bar.

The Natal Society unconditionally apologized for its action 105 years later. It added that the apology also extended to all others "whose access to the profession was restricted in any way on the basis of racial grounds."

An apology can right the wrong of racial and ethnic prejudice and stereotyping.

In passing judgment on another you condemn yourself. (Romans 2:1)

I am sorry for having offended You and Yours, Father.

A Lesson in Achieving

It's not that Lance Armstrong became the second American to win the Tour de France, the world's most prestigious bicycle race. Or that he has won it now two years in a row. It's what he overcame that makes his achievements so remarkable.

In 1996, Armstrong, only 25, and a top pro bicyclist, was diagnosed with advanced testicular cancer. The cancer had spread to his lungs, abdomen and brain. Doctors gave him no more than a 50 percent chance of survival.

However, as Armstrong's mother Linda Armstrong said, "Lance's whole life has been against all odds." He endured four rounds of intense chemotherapy, and after each one-week session he would get on his bike and ride 30 to 50 miles a day.

The cancers disappeared. He married Kristen Ricard in 1998. Armstrong passed up a championship race to be with his wife before the birth of their first child. "You have to get your priorities right," he said.

Through it all, Armstrong says he learned that: "It's not just the convalescence of the body, it's the convalescence of the spirit as well." Words we can all take to heart.

His heart was courageous. (2 Chronicles 17:6)

I believe in Your miracles, Lord.

Seems Like Only Yesterday

What's the difference between history and nostalgia?

According to writer Roy Hoopes, if an event occurred before your time, it's history. If you actually experienced the event, it's nostalgia.

Whether or not you agree with the definition, Hoopes points out an important nuance. Nostalgia by its very nature is personal; history is public.

An example: people now regard World War I as an historical event, yet it represents nostalgia to the millions who actually took part in it.

Memories are precious threads that make up the tapestry of your life. Preserve the monuments and events of your life through journals, photographs and even videos. In years to come, they will be treasured by you and yours.

Do this in remembrance of Me. (Luke 22:19)

Lord, may each and every one of life's experiences bring me closer to You.

Do Unto Others

It can take a whole generation to really understand your parents.

It wasn't until he had two children of his own that Joe Kita began to comprehend the patience and wisdom with which he had been raised.

"My father may have been indifferent about fishing and baseball and many other things he did with me," writes Kita. "But he recognized that the activities connected us and that they were ways to promote confidence, enthusiasm, and drive without ever having to lecture me on these topics."

Kita has discovered that he's not always as enthusiastic as his children are about activities. But, inspired by the many mornings when his father rose at 4:00 am to take him fishing, even though it was only to please his son, he has learned to enjoy watching his children develop their own passions.

Whether it's for a child, a spouse, a parent, or a friend, putting your own feelings aside to support others' interests contributes to a loving relationship.

It is well with those who deal generously. (Psalm 112:5)

Fill us with generosity, Lord.

Helping to Heal a Neighborhood

Go to Best Steak and Gyros House in Minneapolis any morning after 11 and you'll find Sam Riley, Sr. at the table by the window in the back.

From there, Riley can see clearly the parking lot of Chicago Crossings, a small shopping center in the heart of one of Minneapolis' roughest areas. Since Riley's been on the job at that table, the area has gotten more livable.

Riley says his focus is on keeping drug dealers out of the neighborhood and on helping young people realize their dreams.

As a teen, Riley himself had a dream: to be a pathologist. But his family's financial situation prevented him from attending medical school. After high school came a stint in the army. Riley returned home to do battle with the problems of his hometown.

"I didn't go to medical school, but I've helped to make peace in my neighborhood," Riley says. "The work I do here is just as important."

Better is a neighbor who is nearby than kindred who are far away. (Proverbs 27:10)

Give me courage, Master, to be Your instrument this day.

Dead Son Lives on in Mother's Eyes

Nearly blind from glaucoma, Secundina Curtinez was nervous about upcoming eye surgery for a cornea transplant. But the youngest of her nine children, 28-year-old Ivan, was reassuring.

"You will have your eyes, maybe this week," Ivan said, before his sister drove their mother to a doctor's appointment.

That night Ivan unexpectedly collapsed and died of an apparent brain aneurysm. The young New Jersey real estate agent, who had no known health problems, wanted his organs to be donated. His mother was a logical recipient.

Although she would rather have been blind than lose a son, the mother finally agreed to accept Ivan's cornea. The operation was successful. "I saw the doctor's face and I cried," said Secundina Curtinez. "It was a miracle."

Her son's gift to her of sight also reassured her that part of him remains always with her. "Ivancito," she said, "I carry with me."

The fruit of good labors is renowned.
(Wisdom of Solomon 3:15)

May we keep memories of loved ones alive, God.

A Brand New Skirt

Rose Pace sewed a new brown skirt for her five-year-old niece Joan who wore it when her family was invited to dinner at her Aunt Rose's home.

As they were leaving to go home, Joan and her older brother started running hand-in-hand and the girl fell. They were still near their Aunt's house, so they returned.

Joan had scraped her knee and there was a tear in her skirt. Although her knee hurt, she was heartbroken over the tear in her skirt, crying that it was ruined and she would never be able to wear it again.

Joan, who now has five grandchildren, recently reminded her Aunt Rose, "You sewed a brown velvet bow into the skirt where it had been torn, and then I had a brand new skirt to wear!"

Just as one woman used her creativity to mend a skirt and comfort her niece so can we use our gifts imaginatively.

Comfort, O comfort My people, says your God. Speak tenderly. (Isaiah 40:1-2)

Teach us how to use our gifts, Divine Creator.

Faith in the Father

At the end of catechism class, Sister Tomasina told the children, "Father Moschella's father died. We'll go to the funeral parlor." Seven-year-old Anna was concerned. She did not know how the dead looked and was uneasy. None of the other children said anything, so she kept silent.

After they knelt and prayed—Anna at the back—Sister said, "Go into the chapel, shake hands with Father, and wait in the anteroom."

Nearing the doorway, Anna saw none of her classmates frightened or crying. She noticed the shiny black shoes and grey trouser cuffs of the priest's father, and that he looked "ok."

Anna described the visit to her mother, saying that she was fearful of dreaming about it. Anna's mother reassured her, "We'll say an extra Our Father and you won't be afraid."

When dealing with children's fears we can do as Anna's mother did, acknowledge the fears and assuage them.

**'Be strong, do not fear! Here is your God'.
(Isaiah 35:4)**

Loving Father, help us keep the faith we had as children.

Magic Hands

When Dr. Bernard E. Simon died in a New York City hospital at the age of 87, many, including 25 women from Japan, mourned his loss.

Dr. Simon was one of a group of American plastic surgeons who donated his services to help the "Hiroshima Maidens," 25 disfigured and maimed survivors of the U. S. bombing of that Japanese city. They were brought to the United States, where Dr. Simon and others performed a total of 140 operations, rebuilding lips, noses, hands, eyelids and other damaged tissues.

These surgeons also instructed Japanese surgeons in plastic surgery, a field virtually unknown in Japan just after World War II.

Shigeko Sasamori, one of those helped, recalls having been burned over one-third of her body. "Dr. Simon and his colleagues operated on me more than a dozen times," she said. "I was then able to marry and give birth to a son."

New life from the tragedy of war—with the help of people who care.

"Remember now, O Lord...how I have walked before You in faithfulness...and have done what is good in Your sight." (Isaiah 38:3)

Lord, heal our country's wounds.

A Circle of Good Deeds

One day, while Fleming, a poor Scottish farmer, was trying to make a living for his family, he heard a cry from a nearby bog. He investigated and found a small boy mired in the muck. Fleming saved the lad from what would have been a slow, terrifying death.

The next day, a lavish carriage pulled up to Fleming's home. An elegantly dressed man stepped out and introduced himself as the father of the young boy whom Fleming had saved. He offered to pay Fleming for his kindness, but Fleming refused the gift.

Then the man saw Fleming's own son and offered to educate the boy. Fleming agreed. In time, Fleming's son graduated from London's St. Mary's Hospital Medical School and became Sir Alexander Fleming, discoverer of penicillin.

As for the man, his son, Sir Winston Churchill, would one day have pneumonia and be cured by penicillin.

There may come a time when recovery lies in the hands of physicians, for they too pray to the Lord that He grant them success in diagnosis and in healing. (Sirach 38:13-14)

Help me realize, Lord, that You encircle us with Your kindness and compassion.

God Speaking

Have you read or heard about the clever slogans written in God's name by a Florida advertising executive? Here are a few:

"C'mon Over and bring the kids."–God

"We need to talk."–God

"Let's meet at My house Sunday before the game."–God

"Loved the wedding, invite Me to the marriage."–God

"That 'love thy neighbor' thing, I meant it."–God

"I love you...I love you...I love you..." –God

"Tell the kids I love them."–God

These and others may seem flippant. However they remind us that our God is a personal, loving, concerned God; a God who is at once totally Other and deeply in love with each one of us. Keep your ears and heart open.

You are precious in My sight, and honored, and I love you. (Isaiah 43:4)

Remind me, Lord, that our relationship, like any other, takes work. Please give me the strength to cultivate it.

Summer's Special, so Are People

What's summer? A season, you'd say.

If you added, a season of draining heat and humidity and obscenely high electric bills you'd also be correct. But summer is so much more.

It's beach umbrellas and foghorns and lighthouses. It's swimming in the cooling ocean. It's roses on a fence. And farmers' markets bursting with luscious fruits and vegetables in jewel colors.

It's lobsters and corn at a seaside clambake. It's books to read or snooze over. It's yard games. And ice cream in rainbow colors eaten while window shopping on warm evenings.

Summer's also new places and people. Foreign languages and foods. Cultural treasures and modern wonders. Sunburns, blisters and freckles. It's droning bees and winking fireflies. Summer, it's special.

Like summer, indeed like each season, each human being is special. Savor that specialness. Enjoy it. And, thank God for it.

...those who revered the Lord and thought on His name. They shall be Mine, says the Lord of hosts, My special possession. (Malachi 3:16-17)

Help me appreciate, Creator, the specialness of each season and each person.

The Best of Being Human

In the summer of 1999, people around the nation stopped to watch the dramatic television news coverage of a raging fire in Atlanta. Construction worker Ivers Sims was trapped on top of a giant crane.

But thanks to a helicopter crew and a firefighter who volunteered for the mission, the isolated worker was rescued. Hanging from a 50-foot cable, Matt Moseley reached Ivers Sims and delivered him safely to the ground.

Later Firefighter Moseley said, "Nobody gets into this for the money. The reward is helping people. We don't drive Mercedes. The rewards are, when we pass on, we'll leave something behind more than a big house or checkbook."

Whether or not you ever save someone's life, you can change someone's life for the better–today and every day. Take advantage of each opportunity that presents itself to do good. You will find that you are doing good for yourself as well.

Give graciously to all the living. (Sirach 7:33)

You are the source of all goodness, Holy God. Teach me to show Your graciousness to all I meet.

Heritage: a Source of Pride and Self Worth

"The canoe is really the closest thing Canada has to a national symbol," says John Jennings of Ontario. As the founder of what is perhaps the only museum dedicated to the Canadian canoe, Jennings is more captivated by and knowledgeable about the subject than most.

Located northeast of Toronto in beautiful hill country, the Canadian Canoe Museum boasts some 600 canoes that, taken together, trace Canadian history. Its contents as well as its founder help provide insight into the rugged spirit and boundless energy that defines the Canadian national character.

Jennings is proud of his 15-year "obsession" with canoes. He believes that through his efforts, he is doing his part to inspire national pride and unity in his country.

It's easy to see the faults of a nation. What demands passion and commitment is an effort to highlight the blessings of being its citizen.

Nations shall come to your light, and kings to the brightness of your dawn. (Isaiah 60:3)

God, Help me realize the impact that I can make as an individual citizen.

Trading in "the Good Life"

Jim and Jeri Moat could have spent their long-awaited retirement years on a golf course, or vacationing on the Texas Gulf shores.

Instead, they're toughing it out on the unpaved, rocky roads of Arteaga, Mexico, bringing health care education to its citizens.

Delivering much-needed supplies, medicines and information, the Moats travel throughout the three valleys and two mountain ranges. Often, they meet with families living in homes with dirt floors, no running water, and little or no knowledge of disease prevention. "Our main goal is health education," says Jeri.

How do you define "the good life?" For some, there's nothing better than following Jesus.

The Lord has...sent me to bring good news to the oppressed, to bind up the brokenhearted, to proclaim liberty to the captives, and...prisoners...to comfort all who mourn. (Isaiah 61:1-2)

May I have the faith to follow Your lead, Lord Jesus.

Helping Children Face Fears

Faith Tibbetts McDonald writes about how her 6-year-old daughter had suddenly become too afraid to take swimming lessons.

At one time or another, all parents confront similar situations and need to find ways to encourage their growing child to be courageous and take age-appropriate risks.

Tips for a task such as swimming can be adapted to other situations. Some suggestions:

- help the child feel comfortable in the water with you before starting lessons.
- encourage practice.
- take the child to see lessons with no pressure to perform.
- sign him or her up with a friend.
- try not to let your own fears show.

When you think about it, this is exactly what our Father-God does as he encourages us to mature.

To our God and Father be glory. (Philippians 4:20)

Guide parents, Abba, even as they guide their children.

Going for the Gold

Jason Detter returned to his alma mater, McDowell High School in Erie, Pa., for an alumni 5K race. With the assistance of friends who took turns escorting him, the young man who had won a race on the course in less than 18 minutes a few years earlier, began a grueling four-hour journey.

Two years after graduation, Jason spent 19 days in a coma after his car was struck by a tractor-trailer. It was another four months before he emerged from a wakeful but not cognizant coma and began to recognize family members. He also began to regain parts of his memory.

More than two years later, just one month before the race, Jason began walking on his own. He told a reporter he felt ready for the race, and began early so he would finish with the others. He fell nine times during it, but made it to the finish line.

No one in the cheering crowd at the finish line thought he was anything less than a winner.

Not that I have already...reached the goal; but I press on to make it my own. (Philippians 3:12)

God, give us the grace to stay focused on the ultimate finish line, eternal life in You.

A Lucky Life

Freddie Mae Baxter was born into poverty in the South, the seventh child in a family of eight. Her father abandoned the family when she was ten; her mother died six years later.

Moving to New York City, Baxter found work as a cook, a maid, and a domestic. Sharing bus rides later in life with Gloria Bley Miller, who was visiting a mutual friend in a nursing home, she regaled her with tales of her life. Miller, an editor, was inspired to begin recording her stories.

One manuscript and 30 rejections later, Miller found a publisher for *The Seventh Child: A Lucky Life*. Baxter's warmth, optimism, and no-nonsense approach to her difficult life inspires readers to appreciate the goodness of their own lives.

As Nightline's Ted Koppel commented: "Her heart always counts on the world to burst into song."

Do you usually count on the world to sing? Would the story of your life inspire others to appreciate their lives?

Hope deferred makes the heart sick. (Proverbs 13:12)

Guide us, Lord of the Dance, as we move joyfully to the music of our lives.

One Cat, Different Hats

"I do not like green eggs and ham!" is a phrase instantly recognized by most fans of Dr. Seuss (the writer Theodor Geisel).

Geisel devoted much of his life to whimsical prose and illustrations of children's books, bringing great joy to families for generations. Few are aware, though, that Geisel began as a cartoonist for PM, a progressive New York City daily. In more than 400 cartoons, he lampooned Hitler, Mussolini and Stalin among others. He also poked fun at American isolationism before World War II.

"He called 'em as he saw 'em and most of the time he was on the side of the angels," writes Pulitzer-Prize winning cartoonist Art Spiegelman.

Although he eventually found fame and fortune as a children's author, many of these books were actually social commentary on, for example environmental preservation (*The Lorax*) and racial tolerance (*The Sneetches*).

Dr. Seuss stayed true to his message. That's a challenge for us, too.

**My honesty will answer for me.
(Genesis 30:39)**

Show us, Lord, creative ways to bring Your justice to the world.

The Captain

Pee Wee Reese was a Hall of Fame shortstop and popular captain of the famed Brooklyn Dodgers teams of the 40's and 50's. Besides his skills on the ballfield, he contributed the intangible quality of leadership. Teammate Roy Campanella said, "Everyone would look up to Pee Wee."

Never was his captaincy more tested than when Jackie Robinson broke the major league baseball color barrier in 1947. Reese, a native of Kentucky, stood up for and befriended his teammate, thus setting an example of tolerance.

When, during Robinson's rookie season, a rival team began heckling Reese for playing alongside an African-American, Reese simply walked over to Robinson at second base and put his hand on his shoulder. "He was standing by me," Robinson later said. "I will never forget it."

Our world is a much better place when we are color blind toward others.

The measure you give will be the measure you get back. (Luke 6:38)

Help me to understand, God, that we are all equal in Your eyes.

The Necessities of Life

In these days of conspicuous consumption, it's easier than ever to confuse wants with needs. Many feel they must have the latest consumer goods available or else they simply won't survive.

Jo Lembo's parents didn't have much. They and their three young children moved into a one-room shack in Kalvesta, Kansas, which had no electricity, running water or telephone. A wood-burning stove in the middle of the room was the only source of warmth. A propane-powered refrigerator had seen better days. Clothes were washed in a noisy, gas-powered washing machine, and the kitchen was a freestanding oak cupboard with a porcelain work area on top. Lembo's father worked the fields at night while her mother sat and sewed by the light of a kerosene lamp.

Yet, later in life, Lembo loved hearing her parents talk about the "good ol' days." Her mother said, "We didn't know we had it hard. We had all we needed - each other and a lot of love."

If we take the time to look at ourselves we'll probably find we already have all we need.

Is not life more than food, and the body more than clothing? (Matthew 6:25)

Help me be content when my needs are met, Generous Giver.

Just Hanging Out

Rev. Ted Marconi decided to do something for the teens of Smethport, Pennsylvania. Every Wednesday during the summer he hosts a "hang out" in the rectory's backyard. "Whatever the kids want to do, we do," he says.

Many kids prefer to sit around a campfire and roast hot dogs and marshmallows. Others sit and talk quietly. "We've had a few tragedies this year and some kids want to talk about that," Rev. Marconi says. "We end each night with a prayer."

The community has gotten in to the "hanging out" by donating pizza, cookies, brownies, soda and bags of popcorn for the get-togethers. "People have helped us with everything. We haven't had to pay for anything." He adds, that it's exciting "to see others pick up on this idea. It shows there is a real need for this sort of thing."

Teens, younger children, adults of all ages— need companionship and community. How could you become involved?

If you...know how to give good gifts to your children, how much more will your Father in heaven give good things to those who ask Him! (Matthew 7:11)

Every child is Your child, Father. Help me to love the children in my life with Your love.

No Ifs, Ands or Butts

Michael Moore's crusade against the nation's tobacco industry began not with a bang but with a hoarse whisper. When this attorney general in Mississippi took a telephone call from an old law school buddy, Moore heard the story of a friend dying of tobacco-related heart and lung disease.

Soon after, Moore gathered 20 top lawyers, two world-class whistle-blowers and the attorneys general of 39 other states to join in a lawsuit to force the nation's cigarette makers to bear some of the cost of treating tobacco-related illnesses.

To date, the tobacco industry has agreed to pay $368.5 billion. There are those who say it's not enough.

Criticized for possible political aspirations, Moore, for his part, is content. "We've been guided in this thing," he says. "We had some help from above."

And those of us below can breathe a bit easier.

Make me to know Your ways. (Psalm 25:4)

Your ways, Lord, are truth and justice. Help me always to follow Your ways.

Simply Better

Elaine St. James, author of the successful "Simplify Your Life" series, writes about the experiences of a working mother who decided to slowly rearrange her weekends.

Over time, this wife and mother has been able to free up her Saturdays and Sundays so that she no longer takes phone calls between Friday at 5 p.m. and Monday at 9 a.m.

She accepts no social invitations; she doesn't read the newspapers or watch TV; and she runs no errands. If they don't get run during the week, they don't get done.

The result? She now spends weekends relaxing and enjoying the company of her husband and son. By Monday, the family is ready to face another demanding work week.

A change this drastic may not be practical for everyone. But considering the benefits, find at least one evening each week *just* for your family.

For freedom Christ has set us free. Stand firm, therefore, and do not submit again to a yoke of slavery. (Galatians 5:1)

Help us to embrace simplicity, Father; free us from the constraints we put on ourselves.

When the Flood Came from Above

When you have a book store on the third floor of a five story loft, why would you worry about a flood? You probably wouldn't. But, floods can come down as well as up as T. Peter Kraus and his wife Evelyn discovered. They had spent three decades collecting the rare art books in the workshop of New York City's Ursus Books.

After a day of heavy rain, a clogged gutter on the roof sent torrents of water rushing through aisles of books about such artists as Goya, Delacroix, Pissaro and Toulouse-Lautrec, many, original lithographs. The piles of bloated and water-logged paper was, for a book lover, like seeing a lot of dead bodies.

Particularly painful was damage to a 30-volume set by the French editor Loys Delteil that catalogues 19th-century prints.

"The world is full of books," Mr. Kraus muses. "My wife keeps reminding me of the poor people in Turkey, and that there are always people worse off." True. Perspective is everything.

The fountains of the great deep burst forth, and the windows of the heavens were opened. The rain fell...forty days and forty nights. (Genesis 7:11-12)

God, in You nothing and no one is ever lost.

Thoreau or Not Thoreau

A good teacher imparts a lesson by every word and action. Teacher David Barto, does more, he becomes his material.

In 1974, his English students were less than enthusiastic about reading Thoreau, so Mr. Barto arrived in class one day as Thoreau. In character, he responded to everything as if Thoreau were not a 19th century philosopher-naturalist, but a living person whose ideas are equally alive.

This classroom magic moved to Cape Cod, where, for several years, he has been giving nature tours as Henry David Thoreau. He receives $9 a day in meal money from the National Park Service, and a room.

Barto draws on a wealth of information about the life and times of Thoreau and can go for two hours straight. Everything that happens is improvisational, it is not set, he reacts to questions and events as if they are happening for the first time to Thoreau. It is the highest form of art, and exquisite education.

The crowd was spellbound by His teaching. (Mark 11:18)

Help me to hear You, Lord, and to follow you courageously.

Where Values Prevail

Most likely you've heard about the Amish country, in Pennsylvania. For most, the phrase brings to mind a people rooted in the past.

Yet, have you ever considered the enormous challenge it must be to live without modern conveniences? The Amish do not drive cars, access public utilities, accept Social Security or Medicare benefits, or go to war, since these things directly oppose their Anabaptist values and beliefs.

To some, the Amish way of life is unnecessarily harsh and different in a land of progress and plenty–and sameness. But to the Amish, it's a living out of their values–their living values.

Values demonstrated by action set the greatest example for others. How do you express your values?

Lead a life worthy of God who calls you into His own kingdom and glory. (1 Thessalonians 2:12)

Gentle Savior, Your deeds on earth serve as examples for each of us. Thank You for that holy guidance.

Twenty Years Away

Twenty years is a long time. Or is it?

Think back on your family, your work, your whole life and it can feel like twenty years just flew by. Somehow, though, when you look ahead the distance seems much greater. It is easy to put off your hopes and plans.

Yet, if you don't start turning those desires into realities today, you might look back in another twenty years without having achieved your goals.

Here's what Mark Twain had to say about regrets—and about dreams:

"Twenty years from now, you will be more disappointed by the things you did not do than by the things you did do.

"So, throw off the bowlines.

"Sail away from the safe harbor.

"Catch the trade winds in your sails. Explore. Dream. Discover."

'Lord, if it is You, command me to come to You on the water.' (Jesus) said, 'Come.' So Peter...started walking on the water, and came toward Jesus. (Matthew 14:28-29)

Holy God, keep me open to creating changes for good in my life.

A Scary Moment

You are driving alone along an expressway at night. Your car starts to smoke and skid.

That's what happened to one woman. Julia Gottlieb was able to maneuver her car onto the shoulder. Then, within seconds, help arrived.

"My savior was not only a concerned person, but also a mechanic," she wrote in a letter to the editor of the *Miami Herald*. "He knew immediately from the heavy skid marks that my brakes had locked. With kind words he helped me calm down, find my purse and portable phone (which had been jolted elsewhere) and then waited with me until AAA's tow truck arrived.

"He explained that he just loves people and loves to help them because it makes him feel 'happy inside.' Miami is lucky to have Ramon Calix."

Doing good for others is worth the effort. Feeling good about ourselves is a great bonus.

Clothe yourselves with compassion, kindness, humility, meekness, and patience.
(Colossians 3:12)

Fill me with the desire to be happy by loving my neighbor and You, Lord.

Outdoor Films Revive Community

"I'd do anything for the neighborhood," said 89-year-old John Pente, who lives in Baltimore's Little Italy.

What Mr. Pente has been doing recently is allowing a giant movie projector to operate from a bedroom window in his row house, which overlooks a large blank billboard wall in a parking lot.

Instead of becoming a community problem, the parking lot space is now the site of Friday night open air movies. Hundreds of people gather to enjoy *The Name of the Rose, Cinema Paradiso* and other films.

"The movie idea is great," said Maria Monaldi Oma, who now lives in the suburbs with her family. "It brings the old people back out into the streets, me and my old friends return, and the tourists come in." Local businesses are cooperating to help support the film festival. And Mr. Pente couldn't be happier.

"Ci vediamo al cinema!" (See you at the movies!") has become a neighborhood slogan.

I commend enjoyment. (Ecclesiastes 8:15)

Encourage us to appreciate life's simple pleasures, Lord.

Sojourner Truth's Message

When she was about 46 years old and after her five children were grown, the freed woman Isabella wondered how she would spend the rest of her life. She'd faced hardship and grief. Having struggled to come thus far, she felt the need to change her life. Isabella is known to us today by the name she chose, Sojourner Truth.

A former slave who had seen most of her children sold, Sojourner Truth might have turned against God and become bitter. Instead she became an abolitionist and a woman's rights activist who shared the faith her mother had taught her. People could be cruel, but God was kind. God was forgiving.

Sojourner Truth sometimes spoke to her audiences in song. "I know how fiendish hearts can be that sell their fellow men...I still would have them live; for I have learned of Jesus to suffer and forgive."

A woman who fears the Lord is to be praised. (Proverbs 31:30)

Give us the strength and courage to forgive, Jesus.

Talk about Language

Writing in *Civilization,* David Crystal quotes a Welsh proverb: "A nation without a language [is] a nation without a heart."

It has particular poignancy for Mr. Crystal who has noticed that more and more of his North Wales neighbors speak English not Welsh.

"A language's fortunes are tied to its culture's," writes Mr. Crystal. "Just as one language holds sway over others when its speakers gain power—politically, economically or technologically—it diminishes, and may even die, when they lose that prominence."

Latin, for instance, had its heyday because of Rome's power. English dominates today, along with U.S. influence. Not everyone is concerned about the loss of languages. They believe communication will improve if everyone speaks the same tongue.

According to Mr. Crystal, what isn't in dispute is that "each language presents a view of the world that is shared by no other."

If I speak in the tongues of mortals and of angels, but do not have love, I am a noisy gong or a clanging cymbal. (1 Corinthians 13:1)

May we appreciate the uniqueness of languages and people.

A Pact with God

Eight-year-old Joseph Alvarez had a very rare and advanced form of leukemia.

Then the doctors told his mother, Georgia, that Joseph also had a serious brain infection that required complicated surgery. "I ranted and raved at God, and then finally sank to my knees," Georgia recalls. "I promised God I'd do something special if he'd give me one more year with my son."

Georgia got her wish. The brain infection turned out to be a shadow on an x-ray—a fact discovered before surgery. But one year later, leukemia did claim the life of Georgia's son Joseph.

And so Georgia made good on her promise to God. She founded "Wings of Eagles," a group which provides help and support to families throughout California with seriously ill children.

"Sometimes I can't take it," says Suzie Yates, a single mother of a 10-year-old son with a rare disease. "They just come and sit with me and hold my hand."

Support such people. (3 John 8)

Give me strength, Creator, to face the challenges of this day.

Mute in Manhattan

One Monday morning, Jennifer Pirtle, a New York City magazine editor, woke up speechless—literally. A viral infection was the culprit; several days of silence, the only cure. Pirtle found the experience of being mute a mixed one.

On the one hand, she reveled in her predicament. "My experiences seemed newly saturated—like the shock of Technicolor® after years of watching only black-and-white," Pirtle noted.

But, there were moments of frustration: not being able to talk with a friend during breakfast, not being able to call her parents for a chat or let someone know that she was running late for a scheduled meeting.

These days, with her voice healed, Pirtle incorporates some of her week-long experience of silence into her daily routine: for one hour at work, voice mail takes her messages; her early morning routine now includes journal writing, her silent conversation with herself.

"The silence truly spoke to me." Silence became a golden opportunity.

For God alone my soul waits in silence for my hope is from Him. (Psalm 62:5)

In the silence of this day, help me to hear Your voice, Father; to know Your will.

Getting the Goat

Belle, William, Ingrid, Missy, Nan and Naoko are volunteers. Well, sort of. This team of goats was part of a Tennessee conservation project.

Belle and her friends were signed on to remove invasive weeds and shrubs at the Mt. View Cedar Glade Preserve, a location too close to neighboring houses to use the more traditional clearing methods of fire or chemicals. And human volunteers would have taken too long to cut and pull by hand the weeds surrounding the Tennessee coneflower and other rare plants.

So someone suggested: "Get the goats!" Just point them in the direction of exotic weeds and shrubs and these four-footed farm animals will eat just about anything in their path.

The goats, which are on loan from a local supporter of the preserve, are currently being graded on their grazing abilities for possible future foraging.

Assistance can come from unlikely alliances.

Help us, O God of our salvation. (Psalm 79:6)

Master, help us to use Your unique gifts wisely and creatively.

Fruits of the Earth

It's salty, distinctly flavored, black, green, violet, and more than 6,000 years old. What is it?

Evidence suggests that olives were cultivated in the eastern Mediterranean some 6,000 years ago. Some 2,000 years later, farmers learned to extract a most useful elixir from the olive–its oil.

As the plant spread westward, it became the ancient world's most valued commodity. Phoenician voyagers brought olive cultivation to Greece and Spain, and the Greeks took it to Italy. Today, nearly two-thirds of the world's olive oil comes from those three nations.

In just one, small olive lies a clue to culinary history! Consider the wonder of the foods God has given us to enjoy.

Bring you pure oil of beaten olives for the light, so that a lamp may be set up to burn regularly. ...outside the curtain that is before the covenant. (Exodus 27:20, 21)

Father, I pray for the hungry of the world, and for a way to do my part to ease their burning hunger.

An Ice Cream Family

"It's the best job you can get on the Cape," says Tava Ohlsen. She's speaking of a summer job at the Four Seas, an ice cream parlor on Cape Cod in Massachusetts.

Richard Warren has run the place for 45 years. The young women and men he hires are class presidents, newspaper editors and honor roll regulars from Barnstable High School. They have been handpicked by Warren, the school's retired math teacher and guidance counselor.

He makes indisputably delicious ice cream. But more importantly, he makes family out of staff, welcoming young people onto his business' "team" and into his heart. Warren writes his employees' college recommendations and, when they get to college, often visits them. He even brings ice cream to their weddings. At the last Four Seas reunion, only four former staffers out of more than 200 were not able to make it.

"He's like a second dad," says Jahni Clarke. "I tell him about everything."

We are ambassadors for Christ, since God is making His appeal through us.
(2 Corinthians 5:20)

You have called me by name, Father, to show Your face to a waiting world.

Getting Caught Talking to Yourself

We've all done it and have gotten caught. We're talking about talking to yourself.

Experts say that such solo conversations can reap real benefits: improving memory, enhancing concentration, maintaining motivation and raising self-esteem.

Talking to yourself is particularly helpful if you're afraid or angry or in pain, letting the rational and intellectual part of the mind control the emotional part.

Self-speak is also key to self-esteem. "Hearing the words said aloud can override negative thoughts," says Janet Hurwich, Ph.D., a psychologist in private practice in San Francisco. "Hearing your own positive, assertive voice declaring that you are worthy of that praise helps you to believe in yourself."

So the next time you're feeling frazzled by your mile-long to-do list, dreading a confrontation with your boss or wanting to kick that nail biting habit once and for all, do yourself a favor and have a nice chat with your own best friend—you!

Give yourself the esteem you deserve. (Sirach 10:28)

In the silence of this day, I will listen for Your voice, Father.

The Secret of a Loving Relationship

So you found your true love – and you take that walk down the aisle. Everything is going to be great. After all, you've married your best friend. Maybe.

Lots of things can get in the way of staying friends while being married. But take heart. And follow these friendly practices.

Declare a moratorium on criticism. Just stop. A criticism cease-fire is the most effective way to rebuild a friendship.

Listen and let your spouse know he or she is heard. Each of you would listen to a friend go on and on about a problem. Accord your mate the same kindness.

Be on your spouse's side. Encourage. Defend. Play fair. This means declaring "off limits" comments or jokes in sensitive areas.

When you treat each other like friends, you're also likely to revive the spark of love.

One who forgives an affront fosters friendship, but one who dwells on disputes will alienate a friend. (Proverbs 17:9)

Walk with me this day, Lord. Listen to me. Guide me. Be my Friend.

Defenses Against Stress

Stressed? Harried? Defend yourself.

First, be more organized, less hectic.

- Keep a written appointment calendar.
- Give yourself time for a healthy breakfast at home.
- Make time for daily prayer and meditation.
- Say "no" even to friends' requests.
- Do not multi-task, ever.
- Then get rid of clutter in all its aspects.
- Donate what you've cleaned out of closets, attic, basement, store room(s) to charity.
- Confide your fears, worries, problems, joys and sorrows to a journal.
- Go to bed earlier. Sleep does knit up "the raveled sleeve of care."

Your life is God's precious gift. Don't waste it on stress.

Human success is in the hand of the Lord. (Sirach 10:5)

Holy Spirit, guide my efforts to lead a less frenetic life.

Lasting Generosity

Years ago a young Eastern European Jew sold almost all he owned to buy a necklace. It contained 235 diamonds and 18 emeralds. Then, just before Hitler's armies swept over Europe, he hid it under the tiles in his kitchen floor.

The young man and his wife were arrested and sent to a concentration camp. The wife died. The man survived the war and returned to find the necklace intact.

He emigrated to the U. S., remarried, and raised a family. After his death his son sold the diamond and emerald necklace for $277,500 and gave it to an Israeli hospital that treats the elderly poor. Publicity about the sale brought in an additional $385,000 in donations for the same hospital.

As the saying goes 'generosity can not be outdone'. And that's true of God as well as our fellow human beings.

**A generous person has cause to rejoice.
(Sirach 40:14)**

Teach me, Holy Spirit, to give and not to count the cost.

The Cam's Watching!

According to Spokane school bus driver Pat Doten, "Kids will hop around the bus, hang out windows, jump out emergency exits at stoplights."

Meanwhile Doten, and other Spokane school bus drivers try to drive safely while taking students to and from school.

Bus-Cam, a video camera located over the driver, records up to five hours of mischief while the driver concentrates on safe driving. And in case parents doubt a driver's report, Bus-Cam provides a filmed witness.

While it's unfortunate that technology must be used in this way, it does prevent accidents and improve safety. That's important.

Be sure that technology always remains the servant and not the master.

Strive first for the kingdom of God and His righteousness. (Matthew 6:33)

Help us direct technological developments wisely, Creator.

More Murphy's Laws

Here are more chuckles about life.

Good deeds do not go unpunished.

There is always one more bug. And another. And...

You'll find what you're missing in the last place you look.

You must first prove you don't need a loan before you can obtain one.

If all seems to be going well, you don't know what's up.

When more than one person is responsible for an error, no one will be at fault.

When in doubt, at least sound convincing.

What's good in this life is illegal, immoral or fattening.

Have a good laugh at life's pratfalls. And hold on to God's outstretched hands.

I have inscribed you on the palms of My hands. (Isaiah 49:16)

Holy Spirit, give me the brave wisdom to cling to God.

Getting Into the Mud and Getting Out of It

In Panama's Darién province, Rómulo Emiliani is known as the bishop who gets covered in mud.

Mud is part of the life and landscape during the nine-month-long rainy season in this poor region served by a single dirt highway. Since his arrival in 1988 he has wrestled in the mud to change tires on his car, just as he has wrestled with poverty, malnutrition, crime, inadequate education and services, and uncontrolled logging.

He was one of the local leaders who sought help from the Inter-American Development Bank. A bank executive sees Bishop Emiliani as "devoted to the cause of the most disadvantaged." And "sophisticated...getting society to respond and contribute."

After study and consultation, a loan will fund a development program that takes into account environmental, ethnic and economic issues. ...and pave the highway.

Do what you can, whenever you can to contribute to others' well-being.

Pursue righteousness, godliness, faith, love, endurance, gentleness. (1 Timothy 6:11)

Father, show me how to demonstrate my love for those in greatest need.

Troubleshooting Teen Troubles

"It is not easy to be a teen or the parent of a teen. How do moms and dads know what is "normal" rebellion and what's potentially a sign of a major problem?

Lawrence Bauman, a clinical psychologist and the author of *Ten Most Troublesome Teenage Problems and How to Solve Them,* suggests being on the lookout for danger signs:

- Serious negativity about school
- Being highly secretive
- Telling lies
- Obsessing about weight and self-image
- Having tantrums

Instead of panicking or punishing right away, keep talking; stay objective; avoid anger and confrontations; act like a partner not an adversary; recognize your teen's growing independence; compromise when you can. Hold on to family rituals even if a teen does not fully participate.

Above all keep on loving.

If you love those who love you...do good to those who do good to you, what credit is that to you? (Luke 6:36)

Sometimes it is hard to help those we love. Please guide us, God.

Autoworker's Wise Investments

"I always wanted to better myself, but I came up in the Depression. I had to work."

Matel Dawson never got the education that he wanted, but he has seen to it that many of today's young people have the opportunity. Since 1995, the septuagenarian forklift driver, who often works 80 hours a week, has given away more than $1 million for college scholarships.

For decades, Dawson has invested most of his salary in the employee stock-purchase program where he works. He lives in a modest one bedroom apartment, drives a 15 year old car and spends little on himself. For vacation, he travels to his hometown of Shreveport, Louisiana, to meet some of his scholarship recipients.

He says he is just following the example of his mother, Bessie, a laundress. She made him promise to "give something back" and he simply wants "to be remembered as an individual who tried to do some good."

Can we say the same?

In the memory of virtue is immortality. (Wisdom of Solomon 4:1)

Teach me to be generous, Holy God, as You are generous.

The Choices We Make

We do not just make decisions, in a sense they make us.

Eleanor Roosevelt, in *You Learn by Living*, wrote: "There is scarcely an hour of the day in which we are not called upon to make choices of one sort or another, trivial or far-reaching....What shall I wear? What shall I eat? Whom shall I see? Will I take the road to the left or the one to the right?

"Then come the somewhat bigger choices: What shall I do with my life? How much am I willing to give of myself, of my time, of my love? What kind of career shall I decide on–and why?

"Then come the hard choices: What do I believe? To what extent am I ready to live up to my beliefs? How far am I ready to support them?

"We all create the person we become by our choices as we go through life."

What kind of person do you choose to be?

Choose this day whom you will serve.
(Joshua 24:15)

Holy Spirit, You have chosen me to be Your child and servant. Guide my choices in all things.

Bucking Broncos and Trends

You're not likely to find a member of the Rodeo Grandmas watching old westerns on television. That's because the members of this Washington State organization would rather reenact one–by bucking broncos and roping steer. And yes, its members are grandmothers over the age of 50.

While most people over 50 seek fitness through walking, cycling and golfing, a growing number of seniors are bucking that trend, so to speak, and pursuing new and daring ways to stay in shape. Others are intent on keeping sharp the athletic skills they acquired earlier in life, such as skiing or skating.

What limits do you perceive as restricting you from realizing your full potential? Age? Gender? Economic status? Prejudice takes many forms. With determination and an open mind, you can accomplish anything.

How attractive is wisdom in the aged. (Sirach 25:5)

Break the bonds of prejudice in me, Father God.

Lead the Way

What makes a great leader? Charisma? Presence? How about simply the ability to get your point across?

Former New York Yankees Manager Casey Stengel possessed that ability. In one story, Stengel devised a creative way to enforce players' curfew while the team trained in Florida.

After a late dinner, Stengel handed a baseball to the elevator operator as he headed back to his hotel room. "Do me a favor," he asked. "I want to give this to a kid tomorrow morning. Ask any players who come in after me to sign it, then return it to me at breakfast."

Stengel obtained the signatures of the four or five players who'd broken curfew. He promptly fined each one $50 for the violation.

Leadership involves a multitude of qualities. Which ones do you possess?

A people's leader is proved wise by his words. ...A wise magistrate educates his people, and the rule of an intelligent person is well ordered. (Sirach 9:17, 10:1)

Jesus, in following You, I will lead by example.

Hugs and More for Homeless Animals

One day after visiting a shelter, animal-lover Rae French got an inspiration.

It occurred to French that the "lonely animals in cold, hard cages" needed the same comfort she had been providing for her own cats and those of friends and neighbors. She had crocheted "snuggle" blankets from colorful yarns to create warm nests in which cats and dogs could curl up.

French decided to expand her work and enlist others in starting Hugs for Animals and The Snuggles Project. More than 2,000 tiny blankets have been sent to shelters across the country.

One man said his agency, unable to afford animal beds, had been using newspapers. "Now the cats have something soft...and when they're adopted, the Snuggles go home with them."

There are many kinds of strayed and straying creatures, especially human beings. See in the face of these humans the Face of Jesus Himself. And remember that a kindness to one is kindness to Jesus himself.

Rescue the weak and the needy. (Psalm 82:4)

God, inspire us to use our talents to help our lost sisters and brothers.

Cookie Diplomacy

Anna Griffith wanted a way to touch the souls of residents at a shelter for people with AIDS in Texas. But she wasn't having any luck. That is, until her baking broke the ice.

Griffith, a member of Richland Hills Church of Christ in Fort Worth, had two main reasons for seeking a ministry at Samaritan House. "If Jesus were embodied on this earth he would go there." And, as the mother of an HIV-positive son "I knew I would eventually be immersed in that world."

Since her ministry team had been dismissed as "Bible beaters," Griffith tried something different. Each week she brought in homemade cookies and offered them with a smile. Few refused.

Asked why she was doing this she said. "because God loves you." After two years, Griffith started Bible study with a resident.

Persistence and love do pay off.

Love one another as I have loved you. (John 15:12)

Holy Spirit, inspire our words and deeds.

Youngsters Learning the Hard Way

Parents have the painful task of helping their kids learn that actions have consequences.

What do you do if your child doesn't clean his room or finish the yard yet still wants the privilege of a going out with friends to the mall or the movies?

It might be easy to give in, but it's usually not better. Youngsters need to learn what Dr. Henry Cloud and Dr. John Townsend, writing in *Christian Parenting Today,* call "the Law of Sowing and Reaping."

When a child is irresponsible, the parent imposes appropriate consequences. These might include the "loss of time, money, possessions, privileges or activities with people she values."

The authors say to avoid comments like "I told you so" or "Don't come crying to me now." Better to empathize: "I hate it too when I don't get to do something I had looked forward to."

Train children in the right way. (Proverbs 22:6)

Help parents bring out the best in their children, Jesus.

Change Your Career and Maybe Your Life

Changing careers can be rewarding yet risky business. It helps to have supportive family, friends and colleagues as these three women did.

- Beverly Biehr left education and studied for the ministry at age 55, even though she was told local churches weren't ready for women pastors. Her only regret is "staying in an unsatisfying job for so long."

- Kathy Sheppard switched careers from banking to baking while in her late forties. Her salary plummeted while her self-confidence and happiness jumped.

- Sharon Rockett was a 42-year-old wife, mother and homemaker when she went into the financial services field, earning nearly $60,000 her first year.

Each of these women took stock of themselves and their lives and took a risk on change. They're not alone. Have you ever wondered what it would be like to...?

When you come to serve the Lord, prepare yourself for testing. ...be steadfast...cling to Him. (Sirach 2:1,2,3)

Father, bless our efforts to make positive change.

True Success

Dr. Barrie Sanford Grieff, a psychiatrist at Harvard Business School, often works with top management executives. Due to the intense pressures they experience, many CEOs have developed an interesting coping mechanism for personal matters: "They believe in the magic of postponement," says Grieff.

Executives across the country are beginning to see the toll their one-track focus can take, not only on their own lives, but also on the lives of their families. Vance Brown, head of Gold-Mine Software in Colorado Springs, Colorado, says work can be like an addiction. "You lose perspective," he says. "It's hard to know it's happening."

Brown decided to do something about it, and is setting an example for his employees by giving his family greater priority in his life. "If you talk about it, but you don't live it," he says, "employees see right through that. You have to be a role model."

Strive for His Kingdom, and these things will be given to you as well. (Luke 12:31)

Creator of Life, give us courage to live balanced lives.

Preparing for the Harvest

The Law of the Farm governs in all arenas of life asserts Stephen Covey in his best-selling volume, *First Things First*. He admits to feeling clever for having crammed his way through college. "Then I got into graduate work, a different league altogether," he writes.

Within three months he was in the hospital with ulcerated colitis, after trying to catch up on the education he had missed.

Covey uses this example to help people understand the importance of patient and disciplined nurturing. "Can you imagine 'cramming' on the farm?" he asks. "Can you imagine forgetting to plant in the spring...and hitting it hard in the fall, ripping the soil up, throwing in the seeds, watering, cultivating–and expecting to get a bountiful harvest overnight?"

He challenges his readers to consider how the Law of the Farm might be applied to physical health, to marriage, to parenting, and to building a character of integrity.

What will your harvest be?

You visit the earth and...load it with riches. (Psalm 65:8)

Teach us to nurture Your presence in each season of our lives, Savior.

Easter in September

Edie Clark purchases lilies for the altar of her church each Easter. It's a creative way for her congregation to decorate the church and raise much-needed funds simultaneously.

She deeply enjoys the way the rich perfume of the flowers fills the small building and spills out onto the walkway. Like many others, Clark usually delivers her lilies to special friends after the service.

One year, she says, she decided to plant two of the lilies in her yard, despite the fact that she lived too far north for her garden to sustain them. Summer kept her too busy to pay much attention to the tender plants, but in September, she saw a change.

"The leaves turned a vigorous green with a distinct sheen," she noted. When she caught a mysteriously comforting scent from her garden a few weeks later, she suddenly noticed "the white trumpets, four of them, facing east, broadcasting the fragrance of Easter into the autumn air."

The lilies...neither toil nor spin; yet I tell you, even Solomon in all his glory was not clothed like one of these. (Luke 12:27)

Let us proclaim Your life in every season, Lord!

All in Good Time

Actress Gloria Stuart enjoyed great success on the silver screen in the 1930's starring in such films as *Rebecca of Sunnybrook Farm.*

Over the next three decades she worked steadily, but her career as a printmaker began to take precedence. One day, aged 86, she ignored the phone when it rang in her studio. Later, listening to her messages, she discovered it was a casting director from Titanic.

Stuart agreed to an interview the next day. When she was offered the part of Old Rose two months later she could only say: "It's everything I've ever wanted.

She was later nominated for an Academy Award as Best Supporting Actress. This time her response was, "Finally!"

Stuart did not win the award, but lost with grace. "Now," she said in an interview, "I'm back to printing, hostessing dinner parties...arising when I feel like it...yoga poses...being quiet."

And who knows? Maybe that phone will ring once again!

**For everything there is a season.
(Ecclesiastes 3:1)**

Keep us open to Your surprises and ever full of hope, Lord.

A Bare Display of Support

Some people talk a good game when it comes to showing support. In the case of veteran police detective Jim Kautz, he put the top of his head where his mouth is, if you will.

It was bad enough when Kautz's 18-year-old son Brian was diagnosed with a rare muscle cancer. But when he saw how the chemotherapy was taking its toll on Brian's hair, Jim decided to do something to counter his anger and frustration.

Kautz had his barber shave his head. As word of what he had done spread throughout his small Colorado community, numerous fellow police officers volunteered their locks in a show of support. Ten local firefighters and even one female records clerk followed suit.

Gestures count; just ask the people touched by them. As Jim Kautz said of those who participated in the Great Shave-Off, "I see a lot of ugly heads out there, but a lot of beautiful people."

Let us set an example. (Judith 8:24)

Father, help me be unflagging in my love and support of others.

Challenges for Mrs. C

When a tiny Korean girl walked into Suzanne DeMuth Capobianco's first-grade classroom one September, the teacher knew they were in for a challenge. Little Jane didn't speak a word of English. Capobianco didn't speak a word of Korean.

"By the end of the school year, Jane was reading at top level," says Capobianco.

Mrs. C, as her students call her, is used to challenges. "We have kids who are learning-disabled, but they have talents," she says. "I use a lot of different techniques to try to reach children."

Her efforts do not go unnoticed—or unrewarded. Capobianco's desk is full of letters from grateful parents. One of her classes paid tribute to her by planting a tree in her name in the school courtyard. But the highest praise, she says, is when students call her, "Mom."

Capobianco, the mother of two children, says, "The best thing a child can do is make you feel like you're part of his or her family."

God has sent the Spirit of His Son into our hearts, crying "Abba! Father!" (Galatians 4:6)

Make me Your instrument, Lord. May I bring others hope.

Actions to Live By

As Ted Williams was closing out his career with the Boston Red Sox baseball team, he was suffering from a pinched nerve in his neck—a problem so bad, he explained, that he could hardly turn his head to look at the pitcher.

For the first time in his career, Williams batted under .300, with just 10 home runs all season. Yet he was, at that time, the highest salaried player in sports, making $125,000.

The next year, despite the poor performance of the previous season, the Red Sox sent him the same contract. Williams returned it. "I was always treated fairly by the Red Sox," he said. "Now they were offering me a contract I didn't deserve."

Williams cut his own salary by 25 percent for the next season and raised his batting average by 62 points. He closed out a brilliant career by hitting a home run in his final time at bat. Williams also hit home runs in honesty and fair play.

Honesty comes home to those who practice it. (Sirach 27:9)

Keep me faithful to Your word, Jesus.

Your Business or Your Life

If you are involved in an entrepreneurial enterprise and you're married you need to plan, not only for the success of your business, but also for the success of your relationship.

If you and your spouse are active in the same business, you need to clarify how business decisions will be made, what roles and responsibilities you'll take in business and at home and how to keep the romance alive when you're together 24 hours a day.

If you each have separate businesses you'll be struggling with which business has priority over scarce family resources and a shortage of time together.

If only one of you is active in business, you and your spouse will spend most of the day in radically different universes. You need to ensure that you don't drift apart and that you do maintain a common vision of financial and family goals.

Working for yourselves can work out if you work together.

Let marriage be held in honor by all.
(Hebrews 13:4)

Father, this day, bless the work of our hands.

The Road to Riches: Giving

Leibish Lefkowitz came from a wealthy family in his native Hungary. But after surviving the Holocaust and immigrating to Palestine he'd become so poor he and his wife Dina couldn't afford bus fare to the hospital when their first child was born.

When they moved to Brooklyn, Lefkowitz once again became a wealthy businessman. But he did not die rich. Lefkowitz made a habit of giving his money away.

Since he was a Satmar Jew, an ultra-Orthodox sect that sends its children to private religious schools, he felt compelled to give generously to friends who lacked the necessary tuition for their children.

Importantly, his giving was anonymous: he wrote the family a check and let them handle the tuition.

Charity to others is a way of expressing gratitude to God.

Almsgiving...is an excellent offering in the presence of the Most High. (Tobit 4:11)

Enable me to give freely without seeking recognition, Mighty One of Jacob.

Sailing with Hope

When the USS John F. Kennedy docks in New York City, the chaplain makes arrangements for crew members to volunteer in community service projects.

Covenant House asked that the ship's drug and alcohol counselor, Chief Petty Officer Michael Joyce, meet with some of the residents.

He told them of growing up with an alcoholic father. At eight he began working in a grocery store to help support his family. It wasn't long before he, too, turned to alcohol.

With help from Alcoholics Anonymous, and after 12 years of sobriety, Joyce enlisted in the Navy as a counselor.

He told the youths that they would have to work hard to achieve their goal, but that they, too, could dream and succeed.

One man said that Joyce's message was "the strongest message of hope I've ever heard."

Your world needs you to live hopefully.

Hope does not disappoint us. (Romans 5:5)

Give us the courage and strength to put our dreams into effect, Heavenly Father.

There's A Lot in a Latte

Ever imagine that there's a world of history in a cup of coffee?

In his new book, *Uncommon Grounds,* author Mark Pendergrast steers his readers through the intricate history of the little bean that has had such an impact on the world's economies and cultures.

For example: coffee was important in the world economy as early as 1823; nearly 98 percent of American families, including 15 percent of children between six and 16, were coffee drinkers in 1930.

Sometimes, something so small or commonplace (like coffee beans) can have a powerful effect on the world at large.

Ever consider the effect a friendly "hello" can have on a lonely person? One kind word can make all the difference.

A gentle tongue is a tree of life. (Proverbs 15:4)

May I serve as an example to at least one person today and every day, Lord.

The More Things Change...

Ever think about what a "disposable" society we live in today?

Take soda, for example. In years past, it was considered a luxury item. When people did buy it, however, it was packaged in glass bottles with a refundable deposit. Milk, too, arrived via the milk truck and empty bottles were picked up–a type of automatic recycling.

Even glass jelly and jam jars served as drinking glasses after the contents had been eaten. Tin and plastic were rare. Mason jars were used year after year, even passed to the next generation.

Society has changed, but the need to preserve our environment remains. Keep an eye on ways to protect our precious planet. It's the only one we've got!

The earth and its fullness are the Lord's. (1 Corinthians 10:26)

Creator, I pray all people regard the wondrous Earth You created with respect and care.

The Complexities of Addiction

Film maker Robert Zemeckis, discussed the complexities of addiction in his documentary, *The Pursuit of Happiness: Smoking, Drinking and Drugging in the 20th Century*.

"I thought the so-called drug crisis was something that was...our generation's problem," said the Oscar winner whose films include, *Back to the Future* and *Forest Gump*.

He learned that "the crisis has been going on forever–and actually, the worst period in our country's history was the 1830s...everybody was walking around drunk. The country has been sobering up since then."

Zemeckis argues that society criminalizes drugs used mainly by minorities (opium, crack cocaine) while legalizing beer and cigarettes used by the white majority. But he doesn't think addiction can be legislated out of existence.

A heavy drinker in college who changed when he went to film school, Zemeckis said, "You can't control what is basically a personal journey."

If you have an addiction, get help. If you know an addict, support their journey to freedom.

Do not drink wine to excess or let drunkenness go with you on your way. (Tobit 4:15)

Holy Spirit, enlighten us as we pursue happiness.

The Heart of the Matter

Four years ago, Ellen Mitchell's teen-aged daughter, Stacey, suddenly went into cardiac arrest. She had a rare but deadly genetic disorder which affected the rhythm of her heartbeat. A defibrillator machine might have saved her.

Now it is Ellen's mission to put external defibrillators in schools. At a cost of about $3,000 each, six schools have already received machines.

"I figure if I can get help raising the money, then I can get Miami-Dade to be the first county to have defibrillators in every school," Ms. Mitchell said.

The AHA estimates that of the nearly 250,000 people who die of cardiac arrest each year, 20,000 or more lives could be saved if defibrillators were available to first-line responders such as police, firefighters or teachers.

Ellen Mitchell is turning the tragedy of her daughter's death into triumph. There is usually a way to bring good out of any situation.

Declare how much God has done for you. (Luke 8:39)

My heart is restless, until it rests in You, O my God.

Vocational School in the Andes

Rev. Michael J. Donofrio joined the Missionary Society of St. James the Apostle in 1990 and was sent to the Diocese of Abancay in the highlands of southern Peru to spread the Gospel.

Convents in the area took in homeless girls, but not boys. The local parish owned a small house that was used from time to time by visitors, and Rev. Donofrio began letting a few boys sleep there. Word got around and before he knew it, "we had 30 kids and only two toilets."

With government grants and land, private donations, and aid from the Philadelphia Archdiocese, Casa San Martin, a residential training school for poor boys, became a reality.

Besides practical training, the mostly teenage boys attend local schools and do almost all the housework.

God's missions are close-by and abroad. Where does God need your talents?...your energies...your time?

As you have done, it shall be done to you. (Obadiah 15)

Inspire us, Christ Jesus.

The Family Farm Lives

Family farming in America isn't what it used to be. But it may be too soon to write it off. At the same time that there are fewer farms in the United States, a growing number of women are in farming.

Over the years, Chris Feskos has tended to a husband and three children as well as part of their farm's dairy operation. She's also a lay Methodist minister, a hospice volunteer and an educator.

A survey out of Wayne State University reports that the "typical farm wife" puts in 22 hours of farm chores, 68 hours of housework, and five hours of volunteering weekly.

If skill, devotion, hard work and passion are all that are needed to keep the family farm alive, then we need not fear its demise any time soon.

Come to think of it, those traits are enough to make most any dream a reality.

Do not hate hard labor or farm work, which was created by the Most High. (Sirach 7:15)

God, give us what it takes to keep our dreams alive.

Touched By An Angel

Indiana resident Mary McFall, 75, believes she has a guardian angel in feathered form perched on a tree outside her windows.

McFall first spotted the snow-white dove she named "Angel" shortly after moving into a new apartment. She placed water and bread-crumbs near Angel's tree and each day they vanished. In time, McFall put the crumbs closer to her door and finally inside. The nervous bird ate and quickly left.

Soon, however, the ringed-neck turtle dove "learned to trust me." Now, "as soon as I open the door in the morning, in she comes."

One winter McFall rescued the nearly frozen bird which she had found on the ground. When Spring arrived, she feared Angel would fly away. She didn't.

McFall benefits from the companionship, while Angel gets warmth and a good meal.

Like birds hovering overhead, so the Lord of hosts will protect Jerusalem. (Isaiah 31:5)

Increase our appreciation of the amazing beauty and song of birds, Creator.

Delivering Love–In a Chair

While she was reading an article about wheelchairs and the needy, Linda Smith of Harlan, Iowa, decided to become a matchmaker.

It wasn't just learning that many of the disabled living in devastating poverty could never hope to obtain a wheelchair. It was that so many North Americans had access to wheelchairs that were no longer needed. Coincidentally, the mother of four had been looking for a Bible school project for her church, and here it was: to find and match unused wheelchairs with needy soon-to-be recipients around the world.

Her team's efforts paid off. The group succeeded in locating 50 wheelchairs for donation to a worldwide organization that gives wheelchairs to the needy. "It seemed unrealistic for our small church in our little town in rural Iowa," Smith says. "We can't wait to see what God will do next!"

What began as a thought while reading an article resulted in a group effort helping others around the world. One person really can make a difference.

Let your light shine before others, so that they may see your good works. (Matthew 5:16)

Although I am just one person, God, I am important. Teach me to value myself as well as the contributions I can make.

Physician Divine

One of the more obscure and lovely names for God is 'The Divine Physician.' Poetic license, you say. Not really. The fourth study in two years has proven the truth behind the title.

4,000 mostly conservative Protestant North Carolinians over age 64, living in one urban and four rural counties were tested over a six year period.

Those who worshiped at least weekly had more confidants and a larger support network. Physically and mentally they were healthier. And they lived in a more health-enhancing way.

Even when all variables were considered, regular worshippers were 46 percent less likely to have died during the six years of the study.

These findings shouldn't surprise us. A relationship with God through worship, the best and most honest relationship possible, is bound to have profound positive effects on our health and well-being. No other Friend is stronger or wiser.

The Lord will keep you from all evil.
(Psalm 121:7)

Thank You, Divine Physician, for Your friendship and care.

The Appeal of Francis and Assisi

Beginning in 1970 Rev. James McNamara found in Assisi, Italy, a place that offered him peace and solace.

And through this medieval town, Msgr. McNamara discovered one of its most famous citizens, St. Francis of Assisi.

The young cloth merchant Francis, had been on his way to the Crusades when God called him in another direction. Francis spent the rest of his life as a humble and enthusiastic servant of God.

As he faced changes of his own, Msgr. McNamara said he "asked (Francis) to transform my mid-life questions into enthusiasm for God."

Each time Msgr. McNamara has been to what he calls "lovely Assisi," he has come away "more peaceful and more positive." And more determined to live the Good News of Jesus Christ.

May (I) gain Christ and be found in Him, not having a righteousness...from the Law, but... through faith in Christ. (Philippians 3:8-9)

God, grant us peace.

My Sister, My Friend

Jacinta Chvatal, president of Sisters International, says her nonprofit's annual celebration was "founded on the belief that when women unite with a common purpose, they can do great things."

Nani and Heidi Weiss, who work together in a family-owned bakery and restaurant, attended the event because, as Heidi said, "Things get so hectic, we rarely get the chance to sit down and talk."

Each Columbus Day, Cecilia Vickery and her three sisters who live in cities scattered across the United States, meet in a different location. Their get-together is an annual event. "We're moms and wives and homemakers and professionals," says Cecilia, "but Sisters Weekend is the only time we get to interact as sisters."

Family ties and connections with close friends need to be nurtured just for themselves. Call or send a brief note. Showing your appreciation for each other will help you on your way to doing "great things."

I bow my knees before the Father, from whom every family...takes its name. (Ephesians 3:14-15)

Keep us focused on the most important things in life, Lord.

To Albania With Love

There are moments in our lives when we don't ask questions, we simply act. Sharon Bagalio was deeply moved by pictures in her local newspaper showing ethnic Albanians fleeing their homes.

A working mother on a tight budget, Bagalio didn't have much money for donation to the refugees. Then she remembered that the hospital where she worked allowed employees to cash in vacation days twice a year. She donated 12 hours of vacation and received a check for $310.

She also asked the hospital's CEO to support a vacation donation plan she dubbed the "Give a Day of Play" campaign. The response by hospital employees was so great, Bagalio was able to send a check for over $7,000 to Doctors of the World, a non-profit relief organization.

This generosity has inspired Bagalio to take the program nationwide. How can you be creative with your gift-giving?

A generous person will be enriched. (Proverbs 11:25)

Father, bless our generosity.

The Legacy of Yiddish

"What Jews left behind after the Holocaust was literature and a way of life," says Yiddish scholar Aaron Lansky, founder of the National Yiddish Book Center in Amherst, Massachusetts.

Phrases such as "oy," "chutzpah" and "shmootz" have made their way into our lexicon, but the 1000-year-old lingo isn't just "shtick." It's emblematic of a lost Jewish culture that flourished in Eastern Europe before 1939.

Lansky began collecting Yiddish books while studying for his doctorate. One night he salvaged 8000 books from a Manhattan dumpster. On another, he and others saved 15,000 books from the basement of a demolished building. With almost 1.5 million tomes in its stacks, the National Yiddish Book Center has been dubbed "the Jews' lost Atlantis."

It is wonderful to preserve the literary and cultural legacy of a people. An elderly book donor told Lansky, "Young man, this is what we are leaving to the world."

What are we leaving after us?

The good leave an inheritance to their children's children. (Proverbs 13:22)

Remind me that I belong to something larger than myself, Lord Jesus.

Piecing Together a Prayer

"My quilts are a way of expressing thanks to God for this wonderful gift He's given me," says Sandra Scott.

An award-winning quilter, Scott sees herself as an artist who uses fabric rather than the more traditional media of paint or clay. "Fabrics mix in messy puddles in my studio as I snip and shift to see what they'll do of their own accord," she explains. "I'm merely the facilitator."

When Scott and her husband were new to the Chicago area she was diagnosed with breast cancer. She found strength in the promises of Psalm 91. And she and her husband were overwhelmed by the support of members of their church who offered meals, prayers, and help with doctors' appointments.

To express her deep gratitude, Scott created two quilts which now hang in her church. "(They) are my way of worshiping God, the Supreme Creator, to whom all glory is due," she says.

He will deliver you from the snare of the fowler... the terror of the night, or the arrow that flies by day...pestilence that stalks in darkness... destruction...at noonday. (Psalm 91:3,5,6)

Inspire us, Lord, and help us to see Your Presence in our abilities.

Telling a Tale

Jonesborough, Tennessee, is the home of the annual National Storytelling Festival.

Thousands of storytellers compete with one another in an ancient human skill. Tale spinners from all over the world tell stories about the Deep South, the Yiddish shtetls of Russia, or the Celts of Ireland. The best of them teach as they entertain, allowing listeners to discover more about the culture of their ancestors.

Ken Corsbie is one such storyteller. The Guyanese-born master of dialects says it's a universal thing. "A good teller will work anywhere. You make connections with the audience. You take cues from them; you're watching those eyes."

The key in telling a story is to find a way into a listener's head and heart. That link must be there, according to Corsbie.

Stories connect us to the past and illuminate our present. When we connect our heads with our hearts, we live fully in the moment. That indeed is a worthy goal.

(Jesus) spoke to them in parables. (Mark 3:23)

Lord Jesus, Your story inspires.

Take Note of Smiles

Ann was a working mother. Her husband was good about helping, but a lot of the day's responsibilities, especially for their year-old daughter, fell to Ann. She was often too stressed to enjoy her life.

On one particularly stress-filled day, Ann collected the mail and went up to the couple's second-floor apartment to begin preparing dinner. Among the bills and junk mail was a giant yellow card in the shape of a smiling face. Just the sight of it made Ann smile.

The note added to her joy. A friend was thanking her for all the parties of the past summer that Ann had helped to organize and thanking her too for just being a good friend.

At that moment, Ann caught sight of her daughter, sitting in her high chair, a big smile lighting up her baby's face. Ann placed the card on her refrigerator, so she'd see it each night as she prepared dinner.

A single act of friendship, multiple results.

A friend loves at all times. (Proverbs 17:17)

Dearest Lord, You are the source of all my joy.

Cop-Out or Active Strategy?

If you think that religion and spirituality are for the weak and passive, think again.

Recent studies contradict the notion that religious or spiritual-minded people use God as a "cop-out," or as a way to avoid handling life's pressures.

For example, one study of abused women found that the more religious women in the study were more likely to take active steps to solve their problem through counseling and the like.

Assess your relationship with God. Work on growing spiritually but without becoming either self-centered or self-denying. As Hillel said, "If I am not for myself, who is for me, and being for my own self, who am I?"

Coping with life's difficulties through spirituality is hardly passive. It's challenging, rewarding, fulfilling and gutsy with God at your side!

Protect me, O God, for in You I take refuge. I say to the Lord, '...I have no good apart from You'. ...You hold my lot. (Psalm 16:1-2,5)

Heavenly Father, I pray for the faith to continue to rely on You as my partner.

Passing on the Kindness

Charlene Webb Alton has never forgotten what it felt like to be the "new kid" in school. Despite her mom's reassurances, she was so scared that her knees shook.

Then, as she describes it in *To Teach Is to Touch Lives Forever,* "a pretty woman with spectacles hanging on a string came to the classroom door and took me sweetly and firmly by the hand, and she said, 'Why, you must be Charlene Webb. I am so happy to have you here in my class.'...I believed her with all my heart."

Now a teacher herself, the author makes a point of watching for the students who look "a little extra scared, a little more apprehensive than the other children." She makes sure they know that she will "keep a special eye out" for them.

We influence one another in so many ways. The simplest act of kindness can reverberate for years—and lives—to come. Teach goodness the only way it can be taught. By example.

You also should do as I have done to you. (John 13:15)

Instruct me, Lord.

On the Ball

One of the most thrilling moments in recent sport's history had to be the victory of the American Women's team in the World Cup soccer championship.

Michelle Akers, a charismatic, energetic leader, is one of the inspirations of the team. Akers suffers from chronic fatigue immune dysfunction syndrome (CFIDS), which makes her prowess on the field all the more amazing.

But Akers also marshals her strength in order to work with young girls in soccer camps. She has always been open about a rebellious period during her teenage years, and she is trying to help turn around the lives of other young girls. To her, that is more important than anything she can teach about the game of soccer.

Her commitment to God and her faith, to the message of the Gospel, motivates her as strongly as the need to excel and be the best on the field.

The fruit of the Spirit is love, joy, peace, patience, kindness, generosity, faithfulness, gentleness, and self-control. (Galatians 5:22)

Give me, O Lord, patience in failure, humility in success.

"Good" Jobs Available

Apparently workers who are prepared to "do good" needn't worry about future job prospects.

As always, some people will lose their jobs and need to acquire new skills to keep up with workplace changes.

But writer Brad Edmondson finds good news in his reading of the government-issued *Occupational Outlook Handbook*. There will be jobs for healers, peacemakers and storytellers.

An aging population will seek relief for body and soul meaning jobs for such healers as massage therapists, psychological counselors and religious leaders.

Edmondson sees dispute mediation, growing since the 1970s, continuing: ideal work if you know how to resolve conflicts. Finally, skilled storytellers and entertainers have always been in demand.

It's nice to know that doing good might also pay financial rewards as well as all its other satisfactions.

There will be...glory and honor and peace for everyone who does good. (Romans 2:9,10)

Thank you, Father, for the healers in our midst.

Days to Make a Difference

On one Saturday in October, about 1,700 students and staff from 22 public schools in Minnesota mobilized a food and necessities drive to help senior citizens and residents of South Dakota's Pine Ridge Reservation.

On that same Saturday, operating room nurses in Kentucky honored the wish lists of people with breast cancer; and teens in West Virginia got together to clean up eight illegal dump sites on Buffalo Creek. The occasion: "Make a Difference Day."

Created in 1992, Make a Difference Day is the nation's largest day of volunteering. It is estimated that each year some two million people take part in this day of volunteering and good deeds.

Says one participant, country singer Reba McEntire, who helped with the distribution of 600,000 books to poor children in Chicago: "If everyone took an active part in volunteering in their home, community and school, think of how much better our nation would be."

Imagine the difference if every day were "Make a Difference day."

Clothe yourselves with compassion, kindness, humility, meekness, and patience. (Colossians 3:12)

Lord, help me improve one person's life today.

Believing in Yourself

In speaking with boys and girls you may have noticed that they tend to view how well they do in school very differently.

According to the periodical *Child Development*, starting about the fourth grade, boys overestimate their performance. They attribute failures to bad luck, difficulty of assignments or simply not trying hard enough. Girls usually underestimate themselves and blame failure on personal incompetence.

Researchers find that "believing you are competent can be highly motivating. Conversely, believing that you are incompetent can undermine your motivation, even when it's not true."

Beliefs and attitudes can change our lives. Examine the way you look at yourself. Encourage yourself to be your best.

If I am not doing the works of My Father, then do not believe Me. But if I do them...believe the works. (John 10:37-38)

Spirit, show me how to love myself.

The True Measure of Worth

When the gross national product reached over $800 billion in 1968, Robert F. Kennedy cautioned that the figure did not tell the whole story.

He said that money does not measure "the health of our youth, the quality of their education or the joy of their play." Nor did he believe it spoke to "the beauty of our poetry, the strength of our marriages, the intelligence of our public debate or the integrity of our public officials."

More than three decades later, as the Dow Jones Industrial Average again reached record heights, Senator Bill Bradley echoed those words. "Such numbers are not the measure of all things," he said. "They do not measure what is in our heads and hearts. They tell us little about the satisfaction of a life led true to its own values."

Pointing out the similarity in theme of the politicians' comments, Arthur Schlesinger, Jr. noted that a strong economy measures everything except that which makes life worthwhile.

How do you measure success?

Human success is in the hand of the Lord. (Sirach 10:5)

Help us keep life in perspective, Lord.

Barter for Better Health

A man went to see the head of a Maine hospital to explain that he did not have the money to pay for his son's care.

Franklin Memorial Hospital president Richard Batt adjusted the bill, then asked the embarrassed father, who was a writer, if he could assist the hospital by revising some brochures. Batt was amazed: "It was a transforming experience. This man arrived in tears and left feeling good that he could help us."

Richard Batt wondered if a barter system could help other low-income patients. The hospital board approved a voluntary program called Contract for Care. One couple handled the bill for a difficult childbirth by refurbishing the hospital's lawn chairs and creating a photo album to explain medical care to young patients. Another barterer said that she "used to be ashamed to get all those hospital bills. But when you give back something, you feel better about yourself."

The need to give of ourselves is part of being human.

**Those who are generous are blessed.
(Proverbs 22:9)**

Lord, remind me of all you give me; show me how to give to others.

A Song in Her Heart

Growing up, Roberta Guaspari's parents couldn't afford private violin lessons. "If it hadn't been for the music program at my elementary school, I might never have learned to play," she says.

In 1980, she began providing the same opportunity for her students in East Harlem. Soon there was a waiting list for her classes, and children as young as five became enthralled with the possibilities of classical music.

Budget cuts affecting her program in the early 1990's didn't stop Guaspari. She turned to other musicians, including violinists Isaac Stern, Midori, and Itzhak Perlman for support. They joined her students on stage in a fund-raising concert at Carnegie Hall.

The future of her program assured, Guaspari told one reporter that music addresses the hearts and souls of children. "And that's what I think kids today need the most," she said.

I have seen a son of Jesse the Bethlehemite who is skillful in playing, a man of valor, a warrior...the Lord is with him. (1 Samuel 16:18,23)

Lord, help us to do Your will even when the world makes it seem impossible.

One Link to Success

Sports psychologist Dr. Bob Rotella has worked with clients ranging from golfer Phil Mickelson to the U.S. Olympic Ski Team. But he learned a great deal about the importance of a positive attitude through his work with youngsters training for the Special Olympics.

"I started to understand that if you didn't have someone convincing you that you couldn't do something, you could excel," he told *Golf Digest.*

"Negative thinking can be more powerful than positive thinking," Rotella continued, "because so many people are very blasé about their positive (thoughts)."

Rotella said he makes a deal with athletes who don't put much stock in the power of positive thinking. He tells them, "I won't ever again ask you to be positive in your thinking if you will totally eliminate all negative thinking."

He likes to keep things simple. "Let's assume you're going to win some of the time," he tells his clients. "Now, let's just go play."

Hope does not disappoint us. (Romans 5:5)

Lord, cleanse our minds of negative thoughts, so that we can reach our potential.

If Dad Says 'No,' Ask Grandma

Loving grandchildren seems to come naturally. But guidance from grandparents is just as needed.

And grandparenting with today's complications of divorce and distance can be challenging. Here then some tips for becoming a "grander" grandparent.

- Keep up with social trends and how they affect your grandchildren.
- Join or start a grandparent support group.
- Heal relationships. The divorce rate is climbing to over 60 percent of marriages; families are fragmented. If you have a good relationship with your grandchildren's parents, treasure it. If not, try to heal it.
- Stay in touch by E-mail, phone calls, faxes, letters. Take notes on the conversation for follow-up another time. Visit when you can.
- Teach grandchildren a skill you know well; a life lesson; about God, too.
- Pray with them and for them.

Love one another with mutual affection. (Romans 12:10)

Father, light my way this day.

The Sounds of Silence

Every Tuesday and Friday morning at nine a.m., a hundred or so sleepy teenagers straggle into the austere yet beautiful Friends Meeting House on lower Manhattan's Rutherford Square.

They have arrived for a silent meeting, the traditional form of Quaker worship. No one actually begins the meeting. The silence seems to happen on its own.

And when the silence does fall, it's powerful. The noise of the city outside seems to vanish. Sometimes someone will interrupt with a thought, inspired by the silent meditation. Occasionally, the silence is punctuated by giggles and growling stomachs. Some students study and other students sleep. It's not always perfect silence.

Says one teen. "It's always different. Meeting is sort of like...life." That teen's mother recalls the silent meetings of her teenage years. "To sit in silence in the meeting house is to be somewhere else," she says, "a place where you go to talk to the aspect of the divine in yourself, but in silence, listening."

Be silent before the Lord God! (Zephaniah 1:7)

Help me find the silence, Lord, to make You known this day.

Rebirth of a British Cultural Symbol

After an absence of nearly 400 years, and just 200 yards from its original site on the banks of the Thames River, Shakespeare's Globe Theater opened in 1996 with a four-play season.

The decades-long campaign to resurrect the "Wooden O," as Shakespeare dubbed the Globe, was the work of the late U. S. actor, Sam Wanamaker. Despite resistance from the British cultural establishment, his efforts were successful and the Globe was rebuilt using scholarly and archeological evidence.

All the world is a stage, but in a special way the Globe was Shakespeare's. And the reconstructed Globe helps him speak through his plays to today's world.

Jesus spoke to a particular people in a particular age. What can you do to enable Him to speak to people here and now?

Live in harmony with one another.
(Romans 12:16)

Show us how to make the Gospel of peace meaningful here and now, Holy Spirit.

Museum Honors Designers

Peter Cooper, a nineteenth century industrialist and philanthropist, founded New York City's Cooper Union in 1859. Then and now the school offers a free education in art and design, architecture and engineering.

But Cooper's vision of a design museum didn't come to fruition in his lifetime. Establishing the Cooper-Hewitt Museum for the Arts of Decoration fell to his granddaughters. The three Hewitt sisters acquired collections of textiles, lace, prints, decorative objects and the like.

Today, the Cooper-Hewitt National Design Museum, a part of The Smithsonian Institution, carries on Peter Cooper's dream by sharing design treasures with adults and children; by sponsoring educational programs; and by awarding National Design Awards to outstanding modern designers of everything from furniture to utensils to spaces for living and working.

There are ways to share the beautiful and useful with others. Your dreams and patience are vital.

**I have given skill to all the skillful.
(Exodus 31:6)**

May we value and encourage creativity, Jesus.

The Truth Shall Set You Free

Larry Miller was sentenced to 32 years in prison for a crime he did not commit. Only his family and his lawyer believed he was innocent. But the man who committed the crime knew Miller was innocent. Appeals were exhausted, though Miller had a pretty good idea of whom the actual murderer was.

Miller could have let prison and fate destroy him, or find the faith in God's providence he had long ago abandoned. He chose to cling to God and let go of hate.

At the end of nearly 12 years, the true murderer confessed and the process to free Miller began.

The man who was freed was not the same man who went in. He was a man tested, who held fast to God and His goodness to the very end.

'I know that You can do all things, and that no purpose of Yours can be thwarted.' (Job 42:2)

Redeemer, let me never fail to trust in Your goodness and mercy.

Fatherhood Is Best

Ask a man about the best moments in his life and he may speak of a sports or business accomplishment. He may even talk of the day he got his first car.

But every married man is sure to count being a father as, perhaps, the best part of his life. Says father of three Colin Ungaro, "Of all the milestones in your life, nothing changes you for the better more than having children." Adds his wife Susan, "His passion for their every milestone, every success, exhilarates our family and constantly confirms for me the value of a great dad."

Jim McEwen, father of four, says: "What's become clear to me is that kids miss nothing. Everything you do makes a difference. Take time to talk and play. It takes patience, but the payoff is enormous!"

To nuance an old expression, then, fatherhood is best.

Fathers make known to children Your faithfulness. (Isaiah 38:19)

Father, You created me and You love me, unconditionally. May I bring Your love to others each day.

The Library as Pied Piper

At branches of the New York Public Library, children stand waiting for the doors to open.

Inside, they occupy every computer terminal. More than 100 arrive to hear a story-teller. One year, 56 children signed up for the Summer Reading Club at Staten Island's South Beach branch; the next year, 170.

What accounts for this change? Parental involvement. Parents bring their children, collaborate on reading, and encourage their children. After poor results in citywide reading tests, parents turned to libraries for knowledge and inspiration.

Result? Children are becoming readers and starting to succeed in school.

Whether it's in New York City or the smallest village, when children are winners, everyone benefits. And that's not just for today, but for the future.

(Jesus) was teaching...the good news. (Luke 20:1)

Thank you, O God, for speaking to me through every word.

When You're Young at Heart...

It's been two years since doctors operated on Leona Whitney's aging heart. Yet this 83-year-old's schedule shows that the surgery hasn't slowed her life down one bit.

Three mornings a week, the Philadelphia senior drops in on people from her church who, as Leona puts it, "need a visit." If they're sick, she'll shop for them. If they're sad, she'll sit and chat.

Most afternoons, Leona takes care of her great-grandchildren. When they don't need her watchful eye, the after-school program is glad to have it.

And when a slow day creeps into the schedule, which is not that often, Leona will take a bus ride to "wherever." "I talk to everyone I see," she says. "When you speak, you open yourself up to people. That's what keeps you going."

Says Cheryl Lopes, whose grandson Leona looked after, "Leona reaches out to others. People can't help but love her."

"I'm not old," Leona asserts. "I'm looking forward to getting there though."

Those who live many years should rejoice in them all. (Ecclesiastes 11:8)

Ageless. Timeless. So is Your love for us, Father.

Get the Bugs Out

If you had unlimited resources, what kind of house would you live in?...one with modern conveniences? ...every conceivable amenity? What you wish for, might come true.

Steve Kirsch, the mega-millionaire founder of Webportal Infoseek, spent four years and $10 million building his high-tech dream home in California's Silicon Valley.

Included: a rotating sculpture, cascades in the pool and enough AV equipment to fill an electronics store. But, the house is full of bugs.

The motion sensors in every bathroom and closet don't work. The CD player turns on all the televisions at the same time. The front door opens if there is motion inside; the back door locks. And the garage, window blinds, and auto-feeding fish tank are all "buggy!"

Kirsch is spending $60 an hour for an electrical engineer to debug his house. Meanwhile his wife longs for a simpler home.

More is usually not better.

Send (Wisdom) forth...that she may labor at my side. (Wisdom of Solomon 9:10)

Send me patience, but most importantly, Wisdom, Lord.

Giving Teens a Voice

After San Francisco newswoman, Ellin O'Leary had researched a story on teen violence, she realized that teenagers "were terribly misrepresented and unfairly stereotyped by the media." She wanted to give them a radio mike and say, "Talk—we're listening."

And so Youth Radio came into being. It's a weekly radio show produced and hosted by Bay area teen journalists. Three times a year media professionals and peer mentors run a program in the basics of studio operations and broadcast journalism. The key, says O'Leary, is the ongoing relationship between trainee and adult or peer mentor. "The one-on-one interaction is crucial to the kids' self-esteem."

Gerald Ward, a Youth Radio graduate now attending San Francisco State University, says, "Youth Radio gave me the chance to produce something that stands up in the world, and now I want to pass it on."

You, too, have something worth passing on to others.

The only thing that counts is faith working through love. (Galatians 5:6)

Help me know how important it is to teach and be a mentor, Youth of Nazareth.

The Lovable Orange Orb

Barnesville, Ohio, a small city in the eastern part of the state is home to an annual four-day pumpkin festival.

More than 100,000 people attend the Pumpkin Roll contest; the crowning of the Miss Ohio Pumpkin Queen; the choosing of the Pumpkin Baby; and the weighing-in of King Pumpkin.

They buy pumpkins and pumpkin crafts; eat pumpkin pies, pumpkin fudge and pumpkin ice cream. The uniform of the day runs to orange sweatshirts.

Although Ohio is a top pumpkin-producing state, Barnesville is not a big grower of the orange orb. Nevertheless, the festival has taught residents to admire and honor the 7,000 year-old king of vegetables.

"Orange" you glad the pumpkin exists, especially around Halloween? Pardon the pun, but we humans have an incredible capacity to celebrate. Make time to bring laughter and joy into your life.

Sing aloud, O daughter Zion...Rejoice and exult! (Zephaniah 3:14)

May I appreciate and thank You for all Your gifts, Gracious Giver.

The Making of a Saint

When Pierre Toussaint died on June 30, 1853, St. Peter's Church on Barkley St. in Manhattan, was filled to overflowing. Not surprising for a man who was a respected businessman and philanthropist.

But the 87-year-old Toussaint had been far more. A talented and sought-after hairdresser, his clients came from the city's most well-to-do families. Many also turned to this kind, wise and devout man as a spiritual counselor.

His works of mercy were many. He visited people in debtor's prison, cared for those sick with yellow fever, and educated poor children. He also bought and freed dozens of slaves.

This was a very personal mission. Toussaint had himself been born into slavery. His owners brought him to New York City to escape a slave revolution in his native Haiti.

Throughout the many sufferings he endured, he would often say, "As God sends it." Today, Pierre Toussaint is not only a candidate for sainthood, but also an extraordinary model of compassion and generosity.

The righteous flourish like the palm tree, and...a cedar in Lebanon. (Psalm 92:12)

May I be a faithful steward of Your gifts, Savior.

God, Ghosts and the Afterlife

"Science can't explain human feelings," said one 14-year-old. Added another teen, "Science can't explain things like God, ghosts, what's going to happen after you die."

These answers were generated by a survey of nearly 700 teens in Great Britain that posed the question, "What do kids believe?"

Of that group, 75 percent agreed with the statement, "Science can't explain everything." A large majority, 80 percent, believed that events you dream about sometimes come true in real life. Almost as many, 73 percent, found it likely that some houses have ghosts in them.

While the survey stayed away from traditional religious beliefs, the young people were asked if they agreed with the statement, "There is a heaven."

At 53 percent, the afterlife came in just ahead of life on other planets, proving that seeing is not always a requisite for believing.

Job answered the Lord: "I know that You can do all things, and that no purpose of Yours can be thwarted." (Job 42:1-2)

God, help me to realize that You are always with me.

Shall We Dance?

What are more than 15 million Americans doing in their spare time these days to bring more joy into their lives? According to the United States Amateur Ballroom Dancers Association, its membership has doubled in recent years with 20-somethings to 80-year olds all seeking the same thing: fun.

"It's impossible not to be happy when on the dance floor," shares Ann Smith of the Association, a dance aficionado for more than 20 years. "I've always loved the feeling of moving to music. Ballroom opened up a new world for me."

The appeal takes many forms. For some, it's the challenge. Others find needed social interaction through dancing. Still others welcome the refreshing etiquette that is an integral part of ballroom dancing.

Ballroom dancing presents an enjoyable, healthful challenge and outlet to some. What activity brings joy into your life? Take to heart Jesus' precious words, "That your joy may be full."

Keep My commandments...that My joy may be in you, and that your joy may be complete. (John 15:10,12)

Inspire me, Holy Spirit, to seek joy and beauty in all that I do.

Counseling On the Rocks

Maryknoll Brother Jude Conniff knew his competition well when he embarked on his ministry to mariners and their families in Davao, Philippines. "It's hard for me to just go up to the guys and start talking, and it's awkward for them," said the 60-year old Brooklyn-born brother. So, he resorted to the most logical venue to reach out to the sailors, fishermen and stevedores in his parish. "I thought, why not a bar? Now, they come to me," laughs Conniff.

Serving soft drinks and beer each night at the Stella Maris Center, Conniff can help address the concerns of his clientele, "whether they're at port for a few hours or a couple of weeks," he says.

He stresses one common thread among them all. "All these guys want is for someone to listen."

The path to fulfillment can lead us to diverse and unusual places. Sometimes, we can do the most good in the most unlikely setting.

You used to...go wherever you wished. But when you grow old...someone else will...take you where you do not wish to go. (John 21:18)

Lord God, help me keep my mind open to all opportunities to serve You.

Scientist and Man of Faith

In the process of making his dream a reality, a man of science rediscovered he was also a man of faith.

Writing of his experiences in Guideposts Magazine, Dr. Raymond Damadian says that 20 years ago, the idea that doctors would ever be able to scan inside our bodies was just his dream.

Today, magnetic resonance imaging (MRI) is commonly used to see inside the body and make diagnoses without surgery.

During the ups and downs of his research project, Dr. Damadian ignored all else, including church and family. But relatives kept faith and assured him of their prayers.

When good things started happening, the scientist also began to feel the hand of God.

Now, his faith renewed, Dr. Damadian believes "the true thrill of science is the search to understand a small corner of God's grand design."

God saw everything that He had made, and indeed, it was very good. (Genesis 1:31)

Sustain our faith in You, Creator.

Freedom of Choice

In his time, Franklin Delano Roosevelt was one of the most beloved and hated men.

F.D.R. was loved by many because, though wealthy by birth, he believed in and fought for the rights of, as he put it, "the ill-clad, ill-housed and ill-nourished."

But he was hated too, for his propensity to enact change, as well as the very changes he proposed. He posed a threat to the "old order" of doing things, as well as to the people who comprised that old order, the wealthy and privileged.

In a democracy, one person's hero or heroine is not another's. Perhaps that's part of the beauty of a democracy—the chance to have different opinions about the need for or value of change.

But in a democracy opinions must be expressed. Exercise your franchise. Register to vote. Vote in every election.

Bear the responsibility. (Joshua 2:19)

Make me a better citizen, Lord God, in this privileged and free nation of ours.

Love: a Champion's Heart

For more than a decade, Chris Evert was ranked either first or second in women's tennis worldwide. She earned 18 Grand Slam singles titles, three at Wimbledon.

But it wasn't until her retirement in 1989 that she began to fulfill her lifelong dream through the Chris Evert Charities. Her organization has raised more than $8 million in support of various causes, most notably the Ounce of Prevention Fund in Florida.

For Evert, now the mother of three children, the key factor in the programs she supports is that they allow families to remain together. She believes parents who have struggled with addiction and abuse are motivated by remaining close to their children. Such programs benefit the children as they are strengthened by their parents' love.

Evert's commitment to young people began long before she was a tennis champion. As a child she always donated part of her weekly allowance to support children overseas.

How can you encourage children to be generous?

Give thanks. (1 Thessalonians 5:18)

Lead us to a deeper understanding of how we are connected to each other, Creator.

With a Little Help from My Friend

Many of us turn to friends for encouragement, refreshment and renewal. Yet sometimes we overlook an important source of friendship: our own selves.

Women's Day magazine published a series of letters from readers who had discovered how to treat themselves with tender loving care. Their simple suggestions can easily be adapted by others.

Each night Chris O'Shea writes down ten things that happened during the day which made her feel grateful. Rereading her journal at the end of the week helps her feel fulfilled.

Kelly Skoloda visits her grandmother a few times each week on the way home from work. As she hears about what kind of bread her grandmother is baking or which birds stopped at the feeder in her yard, Kelly feels strengthened. "After the craziness of the day, I'm reminded that what matters most is the people I love."

What can you do to renew your friendship with yourself today?

Support your faith with goodness...knowledge...self-control...endurance...godliness with mutual affection. (2 Peter 1:5,6)

Remind me, Lord, of Your presence within me.

The Big Wheel of Networking

These days, just about everyone knows what a Rolodex is, but did you know that a meticulous engineer named Arnold Neustadter invented it? Or that the largest model, the 6035X, is capable of holding an incredible 6000 cards?

"It turned out to be bigger than I ever thought it would be," said Neustadter, who worked in his family's box-making business before leaving it to pursue his lifework: organizing the American office. The first Rolodex came out in the market in 1950, and was a modification of the already popular Wheeldex. A decade later, Neustadter sold his company for a large sum and devoted himself to philanthropy. But he never lost his passion for efficiency.

The Rolodex has earned its place as a tool of networking and status in the American workplace. Arnold Neustadter didn't reinvent the wheel; he simply modified it and put it to a new and fruitful use. More often than not, a tweak here and there is all it takes to produce positive results.

Lord, how manifold are Your works! (Psalm 104:24)

Perspiration leads to inspiration, doesn't it, Holy Spirit?

When You're too Busy to Breathe

Did you ever want to scream because you felt so stressed? Here are a few suggestions to keep stress under control.

Write it out. An essay a day may just keep the doctor away. In a recent study, asthma and arthritis sufferers who wrote for 20 minutes for three consecutive days about the most stressful event they had ever undergone actually showed significant improvement in their health.

Drive at the speed limit. It's safer–and a step toward a less frantic existence.

Go outside. Spend at least 10 minutes a day in nature.

Above all, reach out to the people around you. "Unless we learn to connect with ourselves and others, no amount of managing or organizing will make us feel good," notes Mary LoVerde, author of *Stop Screaming at the Microwave*. "The question is not, 'What do I need to do next?' but, 'Whom should I connect with?' Allot time for family and friends."

Guard me as the apple of the eye; hide me in the shadow of Your wings. (Psalm 17:8)

Refresh me, Lord, when I am weary.

Who Remembers Flanders Fields?

The poem *In Flanders Fields* reminds us of the futility of war and the tragedy of young lives lost.

Major John McCrae, a surgeon serving in Flanders with the Canadian field artillery during World War I, wrote the poem after 17 straight days caring for wounded and dying soldiers.

The brutal time was made more horrible when Dr. McCrae had to reassemble a buddy torn apart by an enemy shell. And as there were no chaplains, he himself read the burial service for his 22-year-old friend.

It was after this that the battle-weary surgeon wrote his famous poem which begins, "In Flanders fields the poppies blow between the crosses, row on row. ...We are the Dead. Short days ago we lived. ...Loved, and were loved..."

This poem draws our attention to the ultimate sacrifice made by countless men and women who served their nations whether in Belgium in 1915 or, in the years since, wherever their "Flanders fields" happened to be.

Nation shall not lift up sword against nation, neither shall they learn war any more. (Micah 4:3)

One day, Lord, may we know an end to all wars.

A Star Prayer

In March 1982, actress Theresa Saldana stepped out of her West Hollywood apartment— and met up with a man who had been stalking her. He stabbed her 10 times, just missing her heart.

For many months, Saldana endured the pain of healing wounds and intense physical therapy. Today, she frequently visits the sick. "I know...how much those visits mean," Saldana says.

What means a great deal to Saldana is her family, her husband, actor Phil Peters, and her daughter, Tianna, and her faith. Indeed, all those who come into contact with her are influenced by her commitment to her Catholic faith and to prayer.

"When my grandmother was critically ill," says friend Randal Malone, "Theresa came to the hospital every morning and every evening to pray with her. She would tell me, 'It's in God's hands, just leave it in God's hands.'"

"I pray every day," Saldana says, "and I encourage my daughter...to speak with God."

How long, O Lord? Will You forget me forever? (Psalm 13:1-2)

I call to You, Lord. Hear my prayer.

Just What the Doctor Ordered

Students at Harvard Medical School will soon join their peers at Washington University and Johns Hopkins University Medical School as they begin to study their patients' spiritual histories. The Harvard students will be participating in a trend being instituted at almost half of the medical schools in the United States.

The National Institute for Healthcare Research (NIHR) has said, "there has been an explosion of research showing, for the most part, that certain spiritual beliefs and practices are beneficial to health and even can help reduce peoples' risk of developing a number of serious illnesses."

While conceding that taking part in religious and spiritual activities is not a guarantee that people will not become sick, the NIHR does report that "people who are more spiritually committed tend to cope better with and recover faster from serious illness when it does occur."

Say to the Lord, 'my refuge and my fortress'. (Psalm 91:2)

Open us to every good You have prepared for us, Almighty Father.

The Risk of Imagined Safety

A few years ago, a group of men watched a sure bet go terribly wrong. Their gamble involved more than $100 billion, some of the finest minds on Wall Street, and rarefied financial concepts like straddles and spreads. Risk, they believed, had been virtually eliminated.

Virtually. If all had gone as the computer models had predicted, billions of dollars would have been made; instead, because of an historical widening of bond premiums—a risk the bettors had ignored because it was 99.9% unlikely—a company collapsed and the global economy was almost crippled.

The men were blamed for taking too many risks. But the opposite is true. They erred not in taking too many risks, but in seeing too much safety in the one risk they did take.

Each of us has such blind spots, areas of imagined safety, but each of us also has the God-given ability to identify them and to alter our choices and actions for the better.

God, the Lord, is my strength. (Habakkuk 3:19)

Lord, grant me the wisdom to see the risk where now I see only safety.

Do You Hear What I Hear?

Terry Weber never attended church as a child. But after he married, he began to attend services at a northwestern Pennsylvania Baptist church. He found much meaning in the congregation's Bible study. Sixteen years later, Weber says God touched his heart, and he agreed to become a lay-pastor in training.

Weber's calling is to ministry with the hearing impaired. "I wanted to do something for the deaf, so I thank God for this," he says. After preparing the lesson especially for his group, he leads the almost two dozen people in weekly worship, sharing a homily in American Sign Language.

Ryan Schenck, a youth minister at Weber's church, says, "You can do good work, but it's limited until you can train people from that culture to teach and help their own."

Weber understands this philosophy. He has only five percent hearing in one ear.

Say to those who are of a fearful heart, 'Be strong, do not fear! Here is your God'. (Isaiah 35:4)

Let us embrace our uniqueness, Lord, and use it to share Your goodness with others.

A Dog's Nose Knows

A dog is more than human's best friend, it is an invaluable tool in the fight to stop the flow of illegal drugs into this country. Dogs have been blessed with olfactory abilities that are a thousand times better than ours. The United States Customs Service uses these expert sniffers regularly to uncover cocaine, heroin and other illegal substances. They are even using specially trained dogs who can sniff out smuggled U.S. bank notes. Dogs are used to discover hidden explosives and weapons. In times of disaster, they are used to find trapped victims.

Most of the dogs come from rescue centers. They receive 12 weeks of special training focused on developing their sense of smell. Labrador retrievers seem to be the best, as are other hunt and fetch breeds large enough to jump onto cargo and baggage carousels. Their marvelous wet noses can detect contraband masked with more pungent smells. More than just a friend, dogs are furry life-savers.

Faithful friends are life-saving. (Sirach 6:16)

Glory be to You, O Lord, who blesses us with extraordinary friends.

When Is Giving Not Giving?

Charity is praised for being the "queen" of the virtues. St. Paul has wonderful things to say about it's importance. Jesus himself told us not to blow a trumpet when we give. However, He did not say what constituted charity. Charity is not just "giving." Is it charity if something given is unusable, not needed, not even wanted?

These difficult questions face the World Health Organization who have looked at the "charitable donation of drugs" to poor countries, to countries experiencing a crisis. Drug companies take huge tax deductions for donations, but sometimes they are donating drugs which are perilously close to their expiration date, or are simply not needed by the people to whom they were given.

It is a good thing to give. But true charity means that we help others, not just ourselves. Charity is love.

A disciple whose name was Tabitha...was devoted to good works and acts of charity. (Acts 9:36)

God of every good gift, help me to give without thought of personal gain.

Ending a Reign of Terror

So you're having trouble with the boss. He or she is most difficult. What can you do?

First, notes Michelle Cottle, a Washington writer on workplace issues, it's time to gather coworkers together. You should discuss your perceptions of the problem, potential strategies for solving it and possible fallout. But don't let these discussions degenerate into pointless complaining.

Next, start documenting your boss's behavior, says Renze Magid, president of a Pennsylvania-based business issues consulting firm. "Keep a log so you have actual facts," she adds. Then select one person to speak for the group and approach the boss. Keep the conversation professional, about business rather than hurt feelings.

If the boss doesn't seem receptive, bring your case to your company's board. No matter how delicately you handle the issue, however, Cottle notes, "heads may roll." "But if you and your colleagues are committed to your organization and believe in its future, your actions–rational and organized–may be worth the risk," she says.

You were called to freedom. (Galatians 5:13)

God our Father, bless all that we do this day.

Point...Click...Volunteer

You have heard of e-commerce, but what about e-volunteering? Jack Backstrand, president of Impact Online, a non-profit service that matches would-be-volunteers with opportunities over the Internet, has pioneered this concept.

"Why shouldn't I be able to volunteer someplace the same day if I have a couple of hours?" said Mr. Backstrand. He convinced some of the biggest Web names to feature his VolunteerMatch service. Now people all over the United States can find and contact appealing service opportunities with the click of a mouse. So far about 75,000 volunteers have been matched with activities ranging from helping the homeless to planting trees.

More lies ahead. Mr. Backstrand imagines volunteer groups using data from the matching service in direct mail campaigns and large companies coordinating service activities for their employees through special volunteer sites.

Thanks to the vision and effort of one person in harnessing the power of this new tool to connect people, the lives of many will be touched.

As you did it to one of the least of these...you did it to Me. (Matthew 25:40)

Help me recognize my ability to help the needy, Lord.

A Different Kind of Love Story

Hope had come to Los Angeles from New York. She lived alone and buried herself in her work. After two years, she felt as isolated as the day she arrived. Randy was Hope's boss' business manager and best friend.

One day, however, a doctor told him he had cancer. When Hope found out, she thought, "Well, I need a friend – and now, so does he." The two became good friends, with Hope standing by him during his cancer treatment. "I just loved being with him," Hope says. She herself became more confident because of the friendship.

Says her boss: "Before Randy, there had been a cloud following her. Then she met him, and the cloud lifted."

Today, Randy's cancer is in remission and he and Hope are married and the parents of twins, a boy and a girl.

Says Randy, "Even in the lowest of moments, life will surprise you." And when you reach out, often there is a someone reaching right back.

Bear one another's burdens. (Galatians 6:2)

Every day, Lord, I pray You'll be at my side.

Death Takes a Holiday

Marcia lost her dad right before Thanksgiving. "That meal was the most depressing one I ever ate," she recalls. "We sat around, with long faces."

When death comes near a holiday, it doesn't have to steal it away. There are ways to cope.

Discuss past traditions and relive past memories with family and friends. Make changes as necessary. Create a special tribute for the day.

Plan in advance to spend the holidays with someone who will understand.

Balance solitude with sociability. Being alone can renew your strength; being with family and friends can be supportive.

Allow time to cry, to write down thoughts and feelings, to talk things over with someone close, to pray.

Give yourself permission to be happy.

Grief doesn't take a vacation from the holidays, but neither do those who love and truly care for you.

The Lord...will swallow up death forever. ...wipe away the tears from all faces. (Isaiah 25:6,7,8)

Lord, who wept for Lazarus, and comforted his sisters, be with me in my sorrow.

A Warming Gesture

A customer walked into a hardware store, asked about its line of hot-water heaters and selected one. After paying for it, the customer left detailed directions for the next morning's delivery.

The next day the store's delivery truck went to a mobile home. The truck driver was met by a father and his three little girls who knew nothing about the purchase. The driver re-checked his instructions and, finding them correct, asked the man, "Sir, are you by any chance in need of a hot-water heater?"

Somewhat embarrassed, the father admitted that they were. "Then," the driver said, "I'll go ahead and unload it." "That family had endured the beginning of winter without any hot water until that nameless customer walked into our store," noted Ami Reeves.

"Without any desire for thanks or recognition, the stranger simply did a good deed and then vanished into generous anonymity." Not known by name, perhaps, but that stranger's generous spirit will live with that family for years to come.

Faith by itself, if it has no works, is dead. (James 2:17)

Father, I sing Your praises for Your great generosity to me.

Word Warrior

When Navajo artist Carl Gorman died at 90, he was among the oldest of the 400 World War II Navajo "code talkers."

Gorman had spent much of World War II in the Pacific theater. A radio rather than a rifle in his hands, he and other Navajo-American Marines made sure that vaunted Japanese code crackers could not decipher U.S. radio transmissions. They crafted a code based on their native language so that U.S. commanders could issue orders and coordinate operations securely.

What's amazing is that Gorman or any native American still spoke their native languages. Official U. S. government policy as well as church-sponsored mission schools punished speakers of Native American languages. Gorman himself had been chained to a pipe for a week because he insisted on speaking Navajo.

Yet Gorman and other Navajo code-talkers' supposedly un-American language saved lives and help win the war in the Pacific.

Stand firm for what you know, and let your speech be consistent. (Sirach 5:10)

Lord, teach us the worth of every person irrespective of language, race, gender, age, economic status, or religion.

A Sacramental Use of Wine

Rev. John C. Staten is more than a Presbyterian minister and college professor; he is the head of the Field Stone Winery in Healdsburg, California.

You might wonder how a minister became a vintner. When Rev. Staten's father-in-law died, he stepped in to run the winery while teaching at a nearby college. He could not do both, and left teaching in 1982.

Rev. Staten says, "The good life for me has to include elements of the sacred." And the connection between wine and religion runs deep: in Judaism wine is used at weddings, on the Sabbath each week, and at Pesach (Passover); in most of Christianity wine together with bread forms the Eucharist.

Rev. Staten's theology informs and supports his work at the winery, and it, in turn, informs his theology. He finds one job a completion and fulfillment of the other.

Eat and drink sweet wine and send portions...to those for whom nothing is prepared. (Nehemiah 8:9,10)

Father, Creator, help me reverence and enjoy all Your works.

Mystery and Beauty

"People say that what we're all seeking is a meaning for life," writes Joseph Campbell, in *The Power of Myth*. "What we're all seeking is the rapture of being alive. People are so engaged in doing things to achieve purposes of outer value that they forget the inner value."

Robert Ludwig, director of university ministry at DePaul University in Chicago, has gained similar insights from his work with college students.

"For many young people," he notes, "being spiritual is about mystery and coincidence, about the beauty of nature, about compassion, exclusivity, and justice." Yet Ludwig sees that students often ignore the life-giving possibilities of a rich relationship with their church.

Ludwig submits participation in a community of worship is worth a second look.

"The goal is the saving experience of God that transforms, renews, and gives life," he muses. "It is all about experiencing eternity right here and now. Everything else–scripture, doctrine, the ethical code, structures–are but means."

Gather...and cry out to the Lord. (Joel 1:14)

Show me the power of community, Lord.

Using Your Differences

As a young Zapotec Indian in Mexico, Felipe Lopez knew that he was "different." Ridiculed for his inability to speak Spanish, as well as his identity as a Native American, Lopez left school after the sixth grade.

At sixteen and barely literate, he ventured to the U. S. in the trunk of a smuggler's car. Lopez took a number of low paying jobs in restaurants while studying after work. In time, he became a U.S. citizen and earned a college degree.

Now he's pursuing a doctorate. Yet the achievement closest to his heart is his co-authorship of a groundbreaking Zapotec/English/Spanish dictionary.

Unaware of God's plan for our futures, our individual differences can become sources of shame. We neglect or cast aside what's most unique about ourselves rather than using them for growth and self-exploration.

Discover and appreciate your "differences." What you find may show how you can make a real difference for yourself and others.

Bear fruit with patient endurance. (Luke 8:15)

Lord, help me accept my individuality, so that I may appreciate others' and together we can do Your will.

Dreams, Disappointment—and Hope

In 1989 Olympic swimming hopeful Tim Duncan watched despairingly as Hurricane Hugo ravaged his homeland of St. Croix in the U.S. Virgin Islands. Hugo's ferocious winds demolished all of the swimming pools.

The then 14-year-old discovered basketball. Over the next few years he developed his skills. Eventually he won a scholarship to Wake Forest University and a first-pick selection by the San Antonio Spurs in the 1997 National Basketball Association draft.

Duncan's team won the 1999 NBA Championship Title. He was unanimously voted MVP of the 1999 NBA Finals.

Sometimes unforeseen circumstances move us in the direction of God's goals for our good, even though the direction is not our own.

But by having faith in God's vision for us and by grasping it we allow God to strengthen us and heal our brokenness. Too, new dreams and new triumphs will emerge from this.

Whoever does the will of God is My brother and sister and mother. (Mark 3:35)

In my brokenness, Divine Physician, strengthen my hope in Your healing touch.

Questions and Unexpected Answers

Have you ever asked a question and gotten an answer you not only did not expect but which taught you something about yourself?

Don Millsap does marketing research. He brought together a focus group of soybean and rice farmers to get their reactions to different versions of a radio jingle for farm equipment. They sat in a motel conference room in rural Mississippi and listened quietly, most with their heads bowed. Then the researcher asked for their reactions.

After a pause, one man spoke up, asking, "This is all you got to do?"

Millsap later said that he froze, too embarrassed to answer. His sense of complacency was shattered.

It may be natural to concentrate on our own affairs, but it can lead to self-importance. Think about the hard work and the hard lives of so many others near and far. And show your respect.

We regard no one from a human point of view... there is a new creation. (2 Corinthians 5:16,17)

I take myself too seriously, too often. Lord, remind me to look at life from the other person's perspective.

Making Bad Manners a Crime

A wise older friend used to say that if children really learned to respect others and always said "please" and "thank you," they stood a good chance for a happy and good life.

Needless to say, manners have fallen by the wayside in contemporary society, and parents and educators wring their collective hands over what to do to correct the trend among children towards discourtesy and disrespect.

Louisiana State Senator Donald Cravins, whose wife became so exasperated that she quit her job as a middle-school English teacher, has now gone so far as to write and get passed the nation's first Manners Bill.

Cravins' purpose: to instill some old-fashioned civility and respect. He believes that just as you can teach a child to read, so "you teach him manners." He hopes the Manners Bill is a first step towards recapturing what's been lost.

Good manners are not the only mark of a respectful individual, they're hallmarks of the caring, considerate person. Our world and our place in it should never move so fast that we forget good manners, caring, courtesy.

Show every courtesy to everyone. (Titus 3:2)

Father, don't let me forget to show respect for all You've created.

Consumed by Consumption

How do you pursue happiness? If it's through a credit card and a shopping mall, consider this:

In his book, *Consuming Desires: Consumption, Culture and the Pursuit of Happiness,* author Roger Rosenblatt examines our propensity to seek happiness through material things.

Is it a need to express the self? Or an unsatisfied yearning for community and family? Whatever the roots, Rosenblatt's book takes a hard look at consumerism, and its empty promises.

Who you are has little to do with what you have. Your true self is expressed by actions, not things. Think about the ways individuals have made an impact on our world: by writing a novel, founding a non-profit organization, organizing the community for change, all efforts that don't require material wealth.

Life does not consist in the abundance of possessions. (Luke 12:15)

Father, strengthen my ability to focus on You, Your values, as I cope with an all embracing consumerism.

The Hero Cat

Heroism is not confined solely to humans. Animals display theirs in the face of adversity as well.

Take Scarlett, a stray calico cat that carried her five kittens to safety from a burning building. Over the past few years, this tale of the fearless feline who rescued her brood has spawned books, magazine articles and television features.

Karen Wellen, an advertising copywriter, was selected by the North Shore Animal League to adopt Scarlett. As Ms. Wellen says, the cat's pluck and personality can serve as a primer on how to overcome adversity. "Scarlett has a lot to teach us all."

No matter the obstacles, we all have what it takes to act courageously when a crisis occurs. Trust yourself, and your God-given instincts.

Be courageous and valiant. (2 Samuel 13:28)

Help me to be brave and take action, courageous Lord.

A Campaign for Freedom

The fourth-grade students at Highline Community School in Aurora, Colorado, are raising money to help free Sudanese slaves. They've raised enough to free 601 so far. A fourth-grader said, "We have our freedom, they should have their freedom."

The children began their efforts when their teacher, Barbara Vogel, read an article about slavery in the Sudan and Mauritania. The class had just finished lessons on American history and slavery and was deeply touched by the story in the paper. They asked their teacher what they could do about it, and the result was STOP, an awareness campaign. Monies raised are channeled through Christian Solidarity International, a nonprofit human rights organization.

Martin Luther King once said: "The greatest sin of our time is not the few who have destroyed but the vast majority who have sat idly by." In these times, let us all practice humanitarianism. Our world needs it desperately.

Why are you standing here idle all day long? (Matthew 20:6)

Help me to strive to right wrongs, Holy Spirit.

No Second Chances?

Whether or not he would ever get a second chance to live outside of prison, Ellis Stokeley helped others in that direction

In 1998, Mr. Stokeley was one of those to receive a Francis Medal given to "men and women who, through generosity of spirit, service and support, have given witness to the values and ideals of St. Francis."

Rev. Robert Struzynski, o.f.m., said that initially Mr. Stokeley didn't believe he could use his life experiences to help others. Nevertheless, he got involved in the Franciscan prison ministry.

"Serving 25 years to life, Ellis 'Bobo' Stokeley has been an extremely effective role model within the walls of Attica," said Rev. Struzynski. In the process, he has "grown into a mature and deeply human person."

Society stands to benefit when men and women, in prison or out, break the shackles of selfishness, despair, anger and indifference. This is where second chances lie.

If you wish to enter into life, keep the Commandments. (Matthew 19:17)

Merciful One, liberate us.

Signs (and Sonnets) of the Times

"Poetry is an act of peace."

That's what Pablo Neruda believed. Robert Frost thought that "Poetry is a way of taking life by the throat."

Poets Anonymous wants people to experience poetry, perhaps, especially, those who rarely think about it. So in January of 1999 they bought space on more than sixty billboards in Los Angeles and put up excerpts from a number of poets.

The words had an impact. One driver wrote to the Los Angeles Times to comment about coming "face to face with the Charles Bukowski billboard. At a time in my life when everything seems a trial, its message–'What matters most is how well you walk through the fire'–startled me. It seemed to have been put there to speak specifically to me."

If you have not picked up a book of poetry for a while, try it. Let the words speak as you sit quietly and listen to what they have to say.

Our ancestors...composed musical tunes, or put verses in writing. (Sirach 44:1,5)

Language is a great and under appreciated gift. Open my eyes and ears to the magnificent possibilities, Holy God.

Communicating with Your Doctor

According to research from Boston's Picker Institute, one of people's top complaints is that their doctors don't listen to them. Here are strategies to help you communicate with your doctor:

Prepare for your visit by listing your concerns and anything health-related that's happened since your last visit clearly and concisely.

Tell your doctor how much information you want to know about your condition.

Be honest, even if the topic is so embarrassing you need to write it down rather than talk about it. Physicians are trained to help with issues you wouldn't want to discuss with anyone else.

Other tips include asking about any new prescription, taking notes, and summing-up in your own words.

Like all relationships, the one between physician and patient requires care and cultivation. Do your part to "grow" your relationship with your doctor.

Give the physician his place, for the Lord created him. (Sirach 38:12)

Don't let me fear expressing myself, Spirit.

A Gift for Sidney

When Phyllis Westover signed up with Christmas Families, she was assigned "Sidney's" wish list.

She knew "that he's 15, wears size nine socks, 30 x 30 jeans, and wants a boom box and tapes for Christmas."

After a discussion with a teenage clerk, Westover purchased a boom box and a tape by U2. He told her. "They've done fund-raisers for Greenpeace and Amnesty International." (Westover had membership cards in her wallet for Greenpeace and Amnesty International.)

Delivering Sidney's package to Christmas Families, Westover was overcome with gratitude to Sidney for the gift he had given her–finding something unexpected.

That's how it is in life. The unexpected comes and we are changed–hopefully for the better.

The Son of Man is coming at an unexpected hour. (Luke 12:40)

Thank you, Lord, for the many surprises You send us.

For His Parents

The Heisman Trophy is awarded each year to the most outstanding college football player. In December of 1981, as soon as his name was announced, Marcus Allen, thought of his parents at home in San Diego. Allen felt the Trophy was simply an affirmation of the great job performed by his mom and dad throughout the years.

Gwen and Red Allen were hard working, doting parents of six children. One or the other was always there for the kids at every practice, school meeting or church function. They never missed one of Marcus's games, all the while instilling in him a sense of social responsibility.

Although Allen possessed enormous natural talents as a runner, his true secret for success may have come from his dad: he told his son to eat a spoonful of honey every morning. Said Red Allen, "When everyone else was tired in the fourth quarter, Marcus was still going strong. It was the bee honey."

Perhaps, but one thing is certain. Marcus Allen knows the difference devoted parents make in the lives of their children.

What child is there whom a parent does not discipline? (Hebrews 12:7)

Father, help parents and children honor one another.

A Special Christmas Meal

It was two weeks before Christmas and Cindy Love was facing another lonely holiday. Her two grown children would be spending the holiday elsewhere, and she didn't want to fix a celebratory meal for just herself, her husband, and her mother. Having just read a story about a woman who had served food at a homeless shelter on Christmas day, Cindy closed her eyes to pray and heard the Lord say, "You need to feed the hungry, too."

She invited travelers passing by on the freeway near her Texas town to join her for a Christmas meal. As the day neared, Love and her husband and friends prepared dinner in the Church hall. Others volunteered to post signs telling travelers to "come eat with us." Sure enough, people stopped to partake. A storm blew in and the freeway iced over, forcing Cindy and the others to provide lodging as well—"like the stable at the first Christmas," she remarked.

Cindy Love fed 150 people and sheltered 50 for two-days. You never know how much you can do until you're called upon to do it.

She gave birth to her firstborn son...and laid him in a manger. (Luke 2:7)

Show me how to welcome strangers in Your name, Lord.

The Tiffany Touch

Entering a church and gazing at the interplay of emerald greens, dark blues and glowing rubies of Tiffany windows, creates a warm glow within. But while the Tiffany glass adds a spiritual and aesthetic dimension to a church's appearance, maintenance is a burden.

St. James African Methodist Episcopal Church in Newark, NJ has six Tiffany stained glass windows around the altar and a rose window six-foot in diameter.

The New Jersey Historic Trust has given St. James' its largest loan, but a church trustee overseeing the restoration believes that even that will not be enough.

Despite this, St. James Church has vowed not to sell its Tiffany treasures to make ends meet. Its ministry to those in need continues under the shimmering light of the windows.

Spiritual and material sustenance combined with beauty, that is the epitome of a House of God.

God's temple is holy, and you are that temple. (1 Corinthians 3:17)

Your beauty is reflected in works of art, Lord.

Operation Chicken Soup

Next time someone complains about aimless, alienated, uncaring teens, tell him or her about an outreach program in New York City called Operation Chicken Soup.

Once a month teenagers cook chicken soup and make sandwiches and snack packs for the mostly elderly residents of Single Room Occupancy hotels.

Since the program, sponsored by the Jewish Community Center, was started in 1996, it has served an estimated 1200 people. Ten percent of Jews in New York City live in poverty, and to do mitzvah or good deeds to help these poor Jews, as well as non-Jews, is the idea behind Operation Chicken Soup.

The high school students benefit as much as the elderly. One volunteer, Jason McGhee, completed his school's community service requirements but continues to help, saying, "This is the direction young adults should be going."

Giving of our time and talents is the way to go at any age.

Let justice roll down like waters, and righteousness like an everflowing stream. (Amos 5:24)

May I know the benefit of helping others, Lord.

Just a Playhouse Small...

Playhouse—"a small house for children to play in" according to *Webster's 9th Collegiate*.

That used to mean four plywood walls tacked together and a plywood roof painted to resemble shingles. Oh, and a few window openings with scruffy tie-back curtains.

Today it means handmade Victoriana with cedar shingles, wooden shutters, and to-order painting—available over the Web.

Or an expensive fishing shack with hand-hewn beams, a French baking oven and World War I era beds.

Parents can even order gingerbread-y or Gothic-y playhouse floorplans and build them.

But does this allow children to develop and use their imagination and intelligence during play? ...Or impose an adult vision on them? Would Dr. Seuss have "found" the Grinch or C. S. Lewis Aslan had they not been free to use their own imagination during play?

Give your children the best gift of all—the freedom to imagine, to dream, to think.

Train children in the right way. (Proverbs 22:6)

Ensure children's freedom to use their imagination and intelligence, Creator.

Stop before You Criticize

The next time you are about to criticize someone, stop.

Joseph Telushin, author of *Words That Hurt, Words That Heal,* suggests that you ask yourself these questions:

How do I feel about offering this criticism? Does it give me pleasure or pain? If you are looking forward to it, your motives are probably not sincere. If, on the other hand, you are reluctant to do it, your concern for the other person will show through.

Does my criticism offer specific ways to change? Avoid the words "always" and "never." They are one dimensional and demoralizing.

Are my words non-threatening and reassuring? Children are particularly vulnerable. Here's a thought from Johann Paul Friedrich: "If a child tells a lie, tell him that he has told a lie, but don't call him a liar. If you define him as a liar, you break down his confidence in his own character."

Concentrate on developing your own good character and you will have a positive effect on those around you.

Endurance produces character. (Romans 5:4)

Mold me into a person of good character who will imitate You in all things, Spirit of God.

Togetherness—a Christmas Custom

Immigrants to America bring memories of beloved Christmas traditions to their new land. Customs may differ from country to country, but one constant is the desire for togetherness.

When Manuel Benitez and Maria Angeles Ramos came to the U.S., there were few Mexicans in their neighborhood and they missed such traditions as Las Posadas, nine days of candlelit processions going from door to door sharing food and singing carols.

Kenyan Wanyambura Mwambia stresses togetherness with his wife and their two children, not the materialism too often found in U.S. homes. "The big thing is to go to Midnight Mass," he says. "The fact that we are together is enough."

Jacques Noisette, says the custom in Haiti had been to go house to house exchanging presents. But here everyone was too busy earning a living. Now, although his children are "Americanized", he says, "we always try to be together on Christmas Eve."

Do not neglect to...share what you have. (Hebrews 13:16)

Jesus, may we share Your birth with family and friends.

Clean Fuel That Smells Like—Food?

The search for clearer and less-polluting fuel takes many turns, it seems. In Medford, New Jersey some of the school buses are running on "biodiesel fuel" which apparently smells like food.

"It smelled like McDonald's french fries or popcorn, something with butter or oil in it," said one Medford fifth grader. Some of the drivers complain that driving a bus filled with the new fuel makes them hungry!

Rural Medford is part of a government-funded study which is evaluating biodiesel as a possible substitute for petroleum-based fuels. Made of a mix of four parts diesel to one part soybean oil, it seems to reduce emissions but it is costly.

"This fuel is not going to be the answer to all our problems," said head mechanic Joe Biluck. However, there's another advantage to using the fuel. "There are no engine modifications needed, no training needed, no upfront costs, and no special parts." And, you can imagine eating fries while driving.

It helps to remain open to a variety of ideas while searching for solutions to pressing problems.

The Spirit of truth...will guide you. (John 16:13)

Holy Spirit, guide our search for solutions to problems.

Unlocking the Mysteries of Our Minds

The next time you dream about purple elephants or monsters chasing you, you may not want to dismiss them as silly dreams or nightmares. Often, dreams are chock-full of meaningful symbols that can tell us a great deal about the situation we're in.

Some psychiatrists believe that the symbolism in our dreams holds the keys to understanding them. Here's a list of some popular dream images and what they may mean:

Angels: The Greek word for angel means a messenger.

Child: Often a symbol of life.

Music: A source of peace and well-being in conscious life, music may suggest inner harmony.

Water: A strong suggestion of your soul and real self. Lakes, ponds and reservoirs can signal hidden emotions and the unconscious; oceans, the vastness of your unconscious mind.

Symbols in dreams, in literature and in the Bible can help us learn about ourselves. It's not always the obvious that has the greatest impact.

God gave knowledge and skill...Daniel also had insight into all visions and dreams. (Daniel 1:17)

Enlighten me, Jesus, Master.

Working for Love

More than 45,000 babies delivered, including twenty-seven sets of twins, two sets of triplets. On call 24 hours a day. More than 60 years experience. Doesn't require payment if customer cannot afford it. Planned retirement: Never. If midwife Jesusita Aragon had a resume, it would likely sound this.

Aragon has, in fact, delivered 45,927 babies in her lifetime, often without any pay except the immense satisfaction she derives from her work.

"Midwifery comes from the heart," she asserts. "It doesn't make any difference that I'm older, I am still strong. The most important thing is the feeling of what you're doing–your hands feel everything." Aragon has found joy and purpose in her work, rather than looking at it as a means to an end.

Sometimes the most rewarding efforts are the ones we expend without a "payback" in mind. Volunteer your talents and skills. You may be surprised at the joy.

Rachel...had hard labor. The midwife said to her... "you will have another son."(Genesis 35:16,17)

Remind me, God, to focus on what I can give.

An American in Paris

In the time since the French Revolution, trained church choirs have all but disappeared in France.

An American, The Rev. Canon Edward J. Tipton, Canon Precentor at the American Cathedral in Paris, knew this. And knew it would help him, as one of the very few organists-choirmasters in France to get his residency permit renewed.

"The immigration authorities rejected my application at first, saying they had plenty of French candidates for those two jobs, organist and choirmaster," explains Canon Tipton, with a laugh. "We...said 'no', it's one job...and I got my permit."

Mr. Tipton understands the value of individuals working well together: "It just takes one person who doesn't care to mess up a whole performance."

What is your unique combination of talents and abilities? How can you combine them with others for best effect?

Praise the Lord with the lyre...the harp of ten strings. ...play skillfully on the strings with loud shouts. (Psalm 33:2,3)

Spirit, guide my quest for individuality.

The Magic of Flutie

Buffalo Bills quarterback Doug Flutie attended Boston College because it was the only Division I-A program that offered him a scholarship.

Coach Jack Bicknell turned to Flutie during a game in which the Eagles were down by 38 points to Penn State's Nittany Lions. Although even Flutie couldn't turn the game around, he did score a touchdown that started him on his unlikely journey to winning the Heisman Trophy.

Associated forever with his 64-yard game-winning touchdown pass in the last six seconds of a game against the University of Miami, Flutie became the first Division I-A player with more than 10,000 passing yards to his credit.

"Football has helped me understand about taking a challenge head-on," he told writer Brad Young. With that in mind, Flutie, whose seven-year-old son is autistic, has established a foundation that has raised over $1.5 million to support research for the disease.

We all have challenges. It's up to us to meet them.

Be proficient, equipped for every good work. (2 Timothy 3:17)

Help us always to stand by our commitments, Lord.

Hold the Donuts!

Unquestionably, the most popular beverage in the world is coffee. Wrong! It's tea. But coffee IS the most popular beverage in the U.S. The world's largest coffee-consuming nation, we savor about 400 million cups of coffee daily—about one-fifth of all the coffee grown in the world.

This stimulating bean seems to have been brought to Arabia from its Abyssinian homeland by 1000 C.E. By the 16th century, the entire Arab world drank coffee. By the 17th century, the Dutch were growing it in Java; the English in Jamaica; and then Central and South America.

It takes about five years for a coffee tree to bear its first crop, but then it will produce several crops a year for at least 15 years.

But growing coffee is labor intensive. Our challenge therefore is to ensure that laborers at each stage from coffee tree seedling to cup of steaming java labor in safety and dignity at family-supporting wages.

Meeting that challenge is a wonderful way to thank God for the gift of our morning eye-opener.

Seek justice. (Isaiah 1:17)

Lord, may I express my gratitude for Your gifts through justice.

Holiday Gifts for Kids and Parents

The Union Rescue Mission in Los Angeles runs its Christmas Store as a store.

Before the Christmas Store started, the mission's Jan McDougall said she'd watch mothers' faces sadden as their children ran to thank strangers for donated presents. "We took the place of the mom emotionally and that was absolutely contradictory to" building and supporting healthy families.

Now parents shop at the Christmas Store with its department-store-style shelves filled with unwrapped toys, games and clothes. They select two items for each child and wrap them with help from mission volunteers.

"This is a whole new concept for a lot of kids to ask for what they want," said mission employee Dale Fitch, aka Santa. "Because their families have so little, they learn not to ask."

Anna Ortega was happy to be able to give gifts to her children. "I told them I was going shopping and we would have a good Christmas."

Sound families, joy and happiness are the best holiday presents.

Celebrate your festivals. (Nahum 1:15)

Encourage us, Lord, to share Your joy.

Doing Battle with Prayer

Not all war stories are about combat. Take the story of Cadet Mantis–"Praying" Mantis," as he was called by his army buddies because of his nightly ritual of dropping to his knees beside his bunk and saying his prayers.

Apart from those prayers, recalls Harry Paige who served with him, Mantis never talked religion, never preached. It was his simple ritual that spoke volumes.

After a midair collision, Mantis chose to stay with the crippled plane rather than bail out and let it crash in a congested area. Mantis was killed–and Paige, his friend, represented the squadron at the funeral services in Mantis's hometown. There, Paige met Mantis's family–and discovered the source of his friend's deep spirituality.

On the first night back in the barracks after Mantis's funeral, Paige found himself getting out of bed, kneeling down and folding his hands to pray. "It was the only memorial that seemed to fit," Paige remembers.

Lord, teach us to pray. (Luke 11:1)

Lead me by Your example, Teacher, and help me lead others to You.

Navigating the Dark Night

People who experience critical illness, says Joan Borysenko, "die to who they have been and are not yet reborn to who they will be."

Borysenko has studied and learned from cancer patients including her own father. She has found that those who struggle to find meaning in their illnesses often find hope and sometimes healing. The words of a chaplain or a doctor are critical, Borysenko believes –"information that one desperately needs to navigate through this new terrain of the soul."

She also sees an interconnectedness between mind, body and spirit that is critical to healing. "And healing does not necessarily mean cure," she explains. "Healing is living in a mindful, creative, forgiving way. Healing is a right relationship, with ourselves and others and with God."

Speaking about the whole journey, Borysenko assures, "Grace is like a seesaw, you only have to go halfway to tip it. The rest of the way is God's grace."

A highway shall be there...called the Holy Way...it shall be for God's people. (Isaiah 35:8)

When I am brought low, Master, raise my eyes to see Your way.

Solutions to Holiday Stress

Here are suggestions for de-stressing your life.

- The best things in life aren't things.
- Do the best you can and no more.
- Practice being a listener, not a talker.
- A happy childhood is possible at any age.
- Delegate. Delegate. Delegate.
- Balance being and doing; noise and quiet.
- Volunteer.
- Reserve credit cards for planned purchases.
- Do something enjoyable for yourself.
- Make allowances for others' heavy burdens.
- Remember, every problem comes with a gift.

Ultimately life is very good. Live life to the full. Begin now, today.

A tranquil mind gives life. (Proverbs 14:30)

Lord of life, You've given me this day as a gift. May I appreciate Your generosity and use Your gift wisely and well.

Celebrating Another's Holiday

Can you celebrate Christmas if it's not part of your tradition? Or Hanukkah or Kwanza?

Israeli born Brooklyn beautician Elán Keter thinks so.

One year he went to a church shelter to wash and cut hair for free.

The next December, to celebrate Christmas, Keter and his staff washed and cut the hair of formerly homeless women for free.

Another time, Keter and his staff washed and styled the hair of visually impaired and blind students exactly to the children's styling instructions. Some of the children had never been to a beauty parlor. Others had never been to Brooklyn. And a few were just apprehensive.

But at the end Keter said, "The kids were wonderful." He added, "I feel so good."

It's true, in doing good for others we do "feel so good."

Do not neglect to do good. (Hebrews 13:16)

Jesus, help us live Your law of love.

Refocusing Christmas

Brenda Poinsett did not want her children to be disappointed, but she did want to prepare them. There would be few Christmas gifts under the tree.

Bob had been out of work for months and only recently had a new job. There were bills to be paid. She told her sons, "Don't expect much." No one looked forward to Christmas.

So Mrs. Poinsett asked God to help her solve the problem . Realizing that they needed to create warmth in their home, she suggested they have an open house. The boys handed out invitations to people they knew well and others they wanted to get to know at church and school. They helped make cookies and an inexpensive punch.

The Poinsetts also thanked God for Jesus' coming. The family and their three dozen guests enjoyed their time together and a truly happy holiday.

Give your problems to God and you may have something wonderful to celebrate, too.

Show hospitality. (Hebrews 13:2)

Jesus, You are especially welcome when I forget how much I need You.

God's Advertising Campaign?

Imagine you're stuck in rush hour traffic, and the billboard in front of you isn't selling shaving cream or a late model car, but contains a message from God.

Thanks to an anonymous citizen of Broward County, Florida, if you've driven in any one of 40 states recently, you may have seen exactly that. Wishing to remind others about God and the spiritual dimension of life, the individual commissioned a local ad agency to produce a spiritual but non-denominational national ad-campaign "that people could relate to in a 90's kind of way," according to the agency.

Certainly, the ads are compelling. Some samples: "Need a marriage counselor? I'm available.–God"

"I don't question your existence."

"I can think of ten things that are carved in stone."

How often do you think of God during the course of your day? Perhaps giving just three minutes a day to prayer or meditation will put everything else in perspective.

Speak, for Your servant is listening.
(1 Samuel 3:10)

Father, help me focus on You.

Answering a Call to Action

On one December morning in Winnetka, Illinois, Stephanie Harper, 16, was walking to school with a friend when she noticed frustrated drivers honking and maneuvering around a slow, erratic-moving sedan. She ran toward the car and noticed that the driver, Glenview, Illinois, police chief David Kelly, was unconscious. He had suffered a seizure.

Harper reached into the vehicle and threw it into park. Next she checked his airway, as she had learned in a CPR class, and used Kelly's own cell phone to summon medical help. Her friends directed traffic around Kelly's now disabled vehicle. Paramedics arrived, restarted Kelly's heart, and rushed him to a nearby emergency room.

Deputy Chief Brad Weigel praised the actions of Harper and her friends. Kelly himself, now fully recovered, also acknowledges his indebtedness to Harper and company: "Because of those girls, I breathe, I laugh, I love, I work—I thank God I'm alive."

Is it lawful...to save life or to destroy it? (Luke 6:9)

Creator, may others see Your light and love in my every action and word.

Alaska: United Via the Internet

The greatest technological advance of the 20th century may be the Internet. The world continues to become smaller and smaller as the information highway connects everyone, even in the most remote locations.

Alaska, a beautiful state with more caribou than people, is, for example, becoming daily more accessible. There are 600,000 residents in Alaska of whom 73% own computers. Only 40% of homes in the lower 48 states have computers.

Newer and more comprehensive fiber optic phone lines are allowing Alaskans to talk on-line to people anywhere in the world. In remote coastal villages, for example, cooperatives knitting scarves from the soft under hairs of the Arctic musk ox, can sell their products in the global market.

Physicians benefit from on-line digitized X-rays, emergency diagnoses, and resulting financial savings in long distance flights.

The Internet is uniting Alaska to the rest of the world. It has the same potential for us, if we use it intelligently.

We, who are many, are one body in Christ. (Romans 12:4,5)

Help us, through You, to be united to each other.

He's Got Heart

Kwabena Frimpong-Boateng, the son of farmers from Ghana, won a scholarship to Hanover Medical School in Germany.

After studying and mastering cardiothoracic surgery at that school, Frimpong-Boateng left Europe and all its comforts and potential for profit. He returned home to Africa.

Today, Dr. Frimpong-Boateng is hard at work expanding the National Cardiothoracic Center in his nation's capital. He helped establish the center to treat the ordinary Ghanaian who would otherwise die of heart ailments. His Heart Foundation supports that center.

This native son of Ghana recalls that on his first day at Hanover Medical School in Germany he told his instructors of his plans to return home. He wanted to help the people of his homeland, and he also wanted to be with his aging mother, who had raised him alone. His father had died just before his birth.

"Somehow," says Dr. Frimpong-Boateng, "your presence alone is enough to make a difference."

A new heart I will give you, and a new spirit I will put within you. (Ezekiel 36:26)

Father, give me the strength to do Your will.

Twenty Years Away

Twenty years is a long time. Or is it?

Think back on your family, your work, your whole life and it can feel like twenty years just flew by. Somehow, though, when you look ahead the distance seems much greater. It is easy to put off your hopes and plans.

Yet, if you don't start turning those desires into realities today, you might look back in another twenty years without having achieved your goals.

Here's what Mark Twain had to say about regrets and dreams: "Twenty years from now, you will be more disappointed by the things you did not do than by the things you did do. So, throw off the bowlines. Sail away from the safe harbor. Catch the trade winds in your sails. Explore. Dream. Discover."

What do you want to discover in the next twenty years of your life? How will you make it happen?

'Lord, if it is You, command me to come to You on the water.' ...'Come.' So Peter...started walking on the water. (Matthew 14:28,29)

God, keep me open to changes for the good in my life.

Is It Too Late?

Here is a thoughtful reminder that, when it comes to many of the truly important things in life, it is never too late to make a difference. The quote is from the former Prime Minister of Lebanon, Saeb Sallam.

"It is never too late to maintain one's rational judgment;

Never too late to preserve one's courage and composure;

Never too late to comprehend lessons;

Never too late to seek new opportunities;

Never too late to depend on true friends;

Never too late to uphold the struggle for a just cause."

Too often we berate ourselves. We regret not having done more or started sooner to achieve a goal. But we can do something valuable each day, no matter our age or circumstance, to bring God's own goodness into the world.

Don't defeat yourself. It is never too late.

Every matter has its time. (Ecclesiastes 8:6)

Paraclete, keep me from giving up on myself and my mission.

Also Available

Have you enjoyed volume 35 of Three Minutes a Day? These other Christopher offerings may interest you.

- **News Notes**–published ten times a year on a variety of topics of current interest. One copy as published is free; bulk and standing orders may be arranged.

- **Ecos Cristóforos**–Spanish translations of selected News Notes. Issued 6 times a year. One copy as published is free; bulk and standing orders may be placed.

- **Wall or Desk Appointment Calendar and Monthly Planner**–The calendar offers an inspirational message for each day as well as for each month. The Monthly Planner with its trim, practical design also offers a monthly inspirational message.

- **Videocassettes**–Christopher videocassettes range from wholesome entertainment to serious discussions of family life and current social and spiritual issues.

For more information on The Christophers or to receive News Notes, Ecos Cristóforos or fulfillment brochures write:

The Christophers,
12 East 48th Street, New York, NY 10017
Phone: 212-759-4050
Web site: www.christophers.org
E-mail: mail@christophers.org